# PICK UP YOUR POKER GAME

# PICK UP YOUR POKER GAME

## TIPS AND STRATEGIES TO GAIN THE UPPER HAND

### ADAM SLUTSKY

TURNER

Turner Publishing Company

445 Park Avenue • 9th Floor
New York, NY 10022

200 4th Avenue North • Suite 950
Nashville, Tennessee 37219

www.turnerpublishing.com

*Pick Up Your Poker Game: Tips and Strategies to Gain the Upper Hand*

Cover design by Mike Penticost

Art Direction by Gina Binkley

Library of Congress Cataloging-in-Publication Data

Slutsky, Adam.
 Pick up your poker game : tips and strategies to gain the upper hand / Adam
Slutsky.
     p. cm.
 Includes bibliographical references.
 ISBN 978-1-59652-826-0
 1. Poker.  I. Title.
 GV1251.S564 2011
 795.412--dc22

2011009622

Printed in the United States of America
11 12 13 14 15 16 17—0 9 8 7 6 5 4 3 2 1

*This book is also available in gift book format as*
*52 Things To Pick Up Your Poker Game (978-1-59652-591-7)*

For Sammi and Taylor

*If you can't bet, you can't win.*

# Contents

# INTRODUCTION

**P**oker is the hottest game and hobby on the planet, more incendiary than a Martian laser beam. According to gaming experts and marketing analysts, more than 250 million people around the world play poker, which translates to one out of every twenty-seven people on earth. From elementary-school adolescents wagering box lunches and homework assignments, to the old-fashioned Amish betting jars of pickled produce and antiquated farm implements, to financially solvent corporate executives working out their frustrations on the felt, it seems that everyone wants to be dealt in on the action these days.

But understand that poker is hardly a Johnny-come-lately. In fact, some might argue it's been a two-century overnight success. Yet despite being around for decades, the poker "boom" as we know it took place in 2003, when a cherubic accountant from Tennessee, oh-so-appropriately named Chris Moneymaker, won the most prestigious poker tournament in the world, the World Series of Poker's $10,000 buy-in main event, with a then-record $2.5 million first prize.

Almost overnight, online poker sites, as well as brick-and-mortar card rooms, experienced an epic surge of new players. The year after Moneymaker's win, entries to the WSOP $10K main event more than tripled—from 839 players to 2,576. In 2005, entries doubled from the previous year—a whopping 5,619 people. And in 2006, insanity reigned supreme in the poker world when 8,773 players vied for the largest first prize in the history of organized sports— a staggering $12 million.

Suddenly, casinos that had once seen poker as the ugly stepsister of gaming action began installing poker rooms on their properties or hurried to refurbish the ones they had all but forgotten about and allowed to languish. As you'd expect, online poker, the means by which Moneymaker—and many other tournament competitors—gained entry to live events, went through the roof.

New Internet card rooms began popping up like mushrooms in cow pastures, and poker players the world over flocked to them like moths to a flame. Poker magazines (*Bluff, Card Player, All-In, Poker Pro*) began appearing on newsstand shelves. Poker radio programs burst onto the airwaves. And even Hollywood jumped into the fray on both the TV and movie fronts: a slew of poker-themed television programs *(High Stakes Poker, Poker After Dark, Hollywood Home Game)* began airing on mainstream channels (ESPN, Travel Channel, and Game Show Network), and new feature films that banked on the success of *Rounders*—released half a decade before the frenzy—were rushed into production starring major celebrities and focusing on the game.

However, the most significant result of Moneymaker's improbable win, far beyond the new life it injected into the game, was that it proved that poker could be played (and played well) by anyone. Age, color, creed, social standing—all are nonfactors where poker is concerned. And whether you're playing for fun or playing for survival, in a penny-ante home game among friends, or in a major tournament or high-stakes cash game among complete strangers, the competitive nature of poker is one and the same.

And therein lies the reason behind *Pick Up Your Poker Game.* To quote ex–New York Jets coach Herman Edwards, "You play to win the game." After all, you're not sitting down intent on losing. Therefore, you should do everything (legally) within your power to better your chances of emerging victorious. The following 52 tips are a giant step in that direction. Good luck!

# 1 BE A WOLF, NOT A SHEEP

In *Rounders*, the quintessential poker movie and the first real exposure many of today's poker players had to No Limit Texas Hold'em, Matt Damon's character (Mike McDermott) delivered a simple yet all-encompassing statement: "If you can't spot the sucker in your first half hour at the table, then you are the sucker."

To put it mildly, poker is not about learning curves. It's not about posterity, and it certainly isn't about playing for an audience. Poker is about cold, hard cash—winning it and losing it. What's more, poker is not a team sport: it's a solo endeavor—just you against the world (or at the very least, the other players at your table). And when you've got no one else to depend on, you definitely do not want to be the weakest in the bunch.

Although skill is a relative term, especially in a luck-influenced game like poker, there is a world of difference between a novice and an expert. These differences are easy to spot—at least they should be—by everyone at the table. Unfortunately, a so-called newbie won't always readily admit it. And if seasoned players can spot the weak members of the herd, those weak members, out of self-preservation, should realize their own limitations ASAP. Bottom line: whether it's painful to admit or not, less-experienced players have to recognize when they are outclassed. Yet time and time again, in an effort to "learn as they go," or boost their image, a lesser-skilled poker player will sit down with superior players and accept his fate as if it were destiny. This is both illogical and crazy. Worse, it serves no purpose. There are plenty of ways to improve your poker skills—from books and videos to online live tutorials to simply playing more poker with players of the same skill level—but a game where your hard-earned money is on the line and the odds are stacked against you most definitely isn't one of them.

It doesn't matter whether you've got a Bill Gates–sized bankroll or Brett Favre–like competitiveness, nor does it matter whether you're playing poker in a brick-and-mortar casino or in an online card room. The point of the game is to win—to leave the table with more money and chips than you sat down with. Intentionally putting yourself in the role of David against a lineup of Goliaths is akin to tearing your money into little pieces, lighting them on fire, and watching the ashes float away. More often than not, that's exactly what's going to happen. Better to be the shark among the guppies, the player that is heads above the competition. You'll have innumerable opportunities to move up a level in the future; if and when you're ready, a game consisting of more proficient players will surely exist. But in the meantime, find the game where you can rule the roost—or at the very least, stand on even ground.

Unfortunately, some players have no patience. They look to jump into the first game with an open seat without even bothering to analyze the lineup. Others, after determining that they are, in fact, the least skilled at the table, will opt to stick it out, hoping to get lucky, which is, in all probability, the only way they are going to leave the table a winner—or a smaller loser. Over time, those scenarios will not only handcuff you to some degree, preventing you from playing your preferred style, but they will also make you resent the game completely.

Therefore, choose your game wisely. Pretend poker is the food chain: every level provides sustenance for the one above it. Under no circumstances do you ever want to be considered sustenance. So if you can't find a game where you are the apex predator—the top of the pyramid—wait. Have a drink, take a walk, go read a book, but whatever you do, don't sit down and play.

# 2 MAKE MONEY, NOT FRIENDS

It goes without saying that the poker table can be an extremely social environment. Indeed, many friendships—and yes, even relationships—have been sparked during poker games. Some poker pundits are even referring to card rooms as the planet's best new "meet markets." But before you sit down and put your hard-earned money at risk, ask yourself one simple question: What's your priority? If the answer to that question is a new best friend or, taking it one step further, a new significant other, go ahead and treat the session like just another networking opportunity or social event and see what develops. You may get lucky and soon be folding wedding invitations instead of substandard hands. However, if your response to that self-imposed query was heavily laden with dollar signs, then forget about being

"Chatty Kathy" and focus your attention on what's important—the poker game.

Now, just because you've elected to keep your eye on the prize doesn't mean you should adopt the persona of an unfriendly buffoon, closing yourself off to all extraneous interaction (the phrase "you catch more flies with honey than you do with vinegar" comes to mind), but this is definitely one of those times when some measure of tunnel vision will ultimately pay dividends. By focusing on the happenings of the game—your opponents' mannerisms, betting patterns, playing styles, and tendencies—you will undoubtedly pick up key bits of information that together will tell the story of your opponents' abilities (or lack thereof) and, cards notwithstanding, dramatically affect whether you leave the table with more money than you sat down with.

On the flip side, if you are capable of multitasking—that is, engaging in irreverent chitchat and idle banter all while remaining focused and in the moment—you may be able to throw off the steely focus of one or more of your opponents, if only just enough to transform their A-game into their B-game (or at least their A-minus game) and seriously diminish their efforts against you. While this may seem like a devious ploy, all is fair (within reason) at the poker table. Sure, constant chatter on your part is likely to annoy at least one of the seated players—most assuredly one of your neighbors—but (a) there's no rule against talking, and (b) if it causes them to play less than their best poker, that's a small victory alone. Still, psychological poker warfare aside, know when to give the yapping a rest; if other players find you annoying and no one wants you in the game, you're likely to find yourself on the outside looking—and wanting—in.

Outside the action at your table, most card rooms are fraught with distractions: attractive cocktail servers, flat-screen televisions broadcasting sporting events, and wild poker action unfolding on the other tables. Paying even the slightest attention to any of these diversions may cause you to miss a tiny but crucial clue about your opponent that could come back to haunt you later on. As it stands, it is hard enough to consistently pay attention to the doings of all your opponents at the table, any one of which may be revealing something about their game at any given moment. Factoring in less-than-complete concentration on your im-mediate surroundings, you are virtually assured of missing something. So when in doubt, scrutinize, don't socialize.

# 3 LOCATION, LOCATION, LOCATION

As is the case with real estate, location plays an important role in poker. By that, I mean your position in relation to the button—that little white disk (often emblazoned with the word "dealer") that travels clockwise around the table, dictating the order of action. In early position—just after the button—you generally have to play a little tighter and be more selective with your choice of hands, as there are many players still to act behind you. Conversely, in late position—closer to, or actually on, the button—you can open your game up a bit. Play a wider range of hands. Take more chances.

However, that doesn't mean you can't use early position to your advantage. For example, by raising in early position you may, in fact, cause players to fold hands that are actually stronger than your own holding. Or you may flush out a really strong hand—that a player will likely re-raise—giving you the opportunity to fold and lose the minimum, far better than what might have happened if you had seen the flop, hit a part of it, and actually thought you had the best hand.

Another possible benefit of raising from early position is that a player with a better holding will simply call your bet, hoping to trap you on a later street. But if fortune is on your side and you out-flop him, you stand a very good chance of enjoying a hefty payday. For example, let's say he has pocket aces or pocket kings and he believes you have a smaller pocket pair. Rather than chase you away, he lets you see the flop, fully expecting his overpair to hold up. But if you connect and hit your two-outer (there are four of every card in the deck; if you already have two, that leaves two you can catch), thereby flopping a set—in all probability with undercards to his big pair—he will probably not fold his hand, and you will get paid off.

Then again, you could always limp in (simply call the big blind) from early position and try to see the flop on the cheap. Keep in mind you may face a raise from a player in later position, dictating you to fold, thus turning your limp-in into wasted chips. But if you are the kind of player who enjoys playing many hands and has no qualms folding to a show of strength, early position play makes perfect sense.

Early position also has its benefits after the flop. Even if you have a weak hand—one that missed the flop entirely—if your opponent is holding a much stronger hand (such as

Ace-King or any other strong, nonpaired hand) but also missed the flop, an early show of force (a bet) might just win you the pot. Similarly, if your late-position opponent has a small or middle pair, if the flop contains all high cards and you bet out, even if you missed, it will make it exceedingly difficult for him to call, thus giving you the win.

Conversely, playing from late position offers many advantages, the best of which is the luxury of getting to act last, after your opponents have made their decisions. For example, if an opponent wants to trap you, he might check, expecting you to bet, and then he will check-raise. But if you're not sure of the situation, you can always check right behind him and nullify his ploy. Or, if an opponent bets from early position, you can then raise, hoping to get free cards on the coming streets. Your aggressiveness will more than likely cause him to check the next card, regardless of what it is. If it offers you no help, you can also check, essentially giving you two cards for the price of one.

Ultimately, it all boils down to your style of play. Early position, late position, check, or bet—it depends on your plan of attack for that particular hand. Instead of getting locked into a pattern, whereby your opponents will become accustomed to your actions and be able to consistently beat you to the punch, vary your play. Keep your opponents off-balance and constantly guessing. If they can't pin you on a hand, half the battle is over.

# 4 LOOK BEFORE YOU LEAP

Quoting lyrics from a hit 1980 disco song in a book geared towards playing better poker may seem unusual, but trust me, in this case it's wholly appropriate. The hit song in question: "Take Your Time (Do It Right)" by the S.O.S. Band. The lyrics:

Baby, we can do it
Take the time
Do it right
We can do it, baby
Do it tonight

Now imagine those words coming from your own sub-conscious, a self-generated subliminal message imploring you to slow down and think things through before making any rash decisions—decisions where cash and chips hang in the balance. Although it's true that poker is heavily influenced by luck and aggression, it's also an extremely cerebral game, requiring considerable thought at all stages and all skill levels—from bare-bones beginner to seasoned expert. Information is readily available to every player at the table, provided they take the time to look for it and, more important, put that information to good use. And unlike ball sports or other games where a ticking clock plays a major role in the action, poker players have the luxury of time on their side.

Billy the Kid–like quickness is an impressive trait, but at the poker table, it's also an unnecessary trait, one that will hurt you far more than it will help you. On every street, players are given the courtesy of weighing their options. Sure, it's a good idea to have some semblance of what you want to do when it's your turn, but depending upon the action of the preceding players, your predetermined strategy may (and should) change, thus requiring some last-minute, in-depth contemplation.

Players who repeatedly abuse this generous allotment of time (often referred to as Hollywooding) may find other players calling the clock on them, which involves a floorman being dispatched to impose a strict time limit for decisions, the penalty for violators being a dead hand. But in most cases, a reasonable length of time (longer when a particularly large pot is on the line) will be extended.

Players should put this time to good use. Focus not on the here and now but on all the events leading up to your turn—events from the last hand and previous hands throughout the session. Replay the action in your head. Try to recall any information you have about each player. And most of all, put yourself in your opponent's shoes and get a read on both the situation and your opponent's hand.

Finally, because time is on your side, don't tip off other players as to your intended course of action by visibly preparing to act before it's your turn. For example, even if you know you are going to fold, don't have your cards up and ready to be tossed into the muck until your turn arrives. The same advice applies whether you are preparing to bet, call, or raise—leave your chips on the table until it's your action. If you know what a player following you is going to do, that clue will greatly influence your decision. It may help you get the correct pot odds for staying in, or it may allow you to save money and chips and get out of the way if a player is intending to raise.

# 5 YOU SHOULDN'T SHOP FOR CHAMPAGNE IF YOU ARE ON A BEER BUDGET

**D**eath and taxes are the absolutes of life. Unfortunately, there are no absolutes in poker. The best player on the planet is still susceptible to the worst player at any given time. Granted, the odds may be seriously stacked in the better player's favor, but because poker is a form of gambling, and all forms of gambling share the commonality of luck, even the proposition with the longest of odds will eventually come in. Having said that, it's imperative that poker players never play outside their financial comfort zone. In layman's terms: never play with more than you can afford to lose. Yet poker players around the world—even those who are very experienced, exceptionally talented, and fully cognizant of the game's peaks and valleys—are constantly crossing that line, often with dire consequences.

Consider the expert tightrope walker who always works without a net. Ninety-nine times out of a hundred he's going to make that traverse with nary a hitch. But that one hundredth time—*splat!* Game over. Losing a buy-in or two is one thing. But losing the money that puts clothes on your back, food in your belly, or a roof over your head is an entirely different kettle of fish. And if you happen to have other responsibilities—obligations in the form of a spouse or children (or both), you're not just playing with your money—you're playing with their lives.

Just as it is with all other forms of gambling, the prospect of turning a small stake into a larger one is among poker's greatest draws. Sitting down with a little and getting up with a lot is every poker player's goal. And despite the insurmountable evidence that poker is indeed a skill game, one cannot argue with the role luck plays—otherwise the innumerable tournaments held around the world would have the exact same faces at their final tables. It's for that reason alone that risking potentially devastating scenarios—i.e., the loss of your fiscal safety net—should be avoided at all costs.

One does not need to play poker at the so-called nosebleed levels to enjoy the game. The competitive aspects remain unchanged regardless of the stakes. Should you find yourself gravitating to games where fortune or famine hangs on the turn of every card, I suggest you quit poker altogether. Sooner or later, your luck will run out.

A good way of determining the best stakes for you is

to employ the 50-1 Rule. Simply put, this means avoiding games where the usual buy-in is greater than 50 times your cash reserves. For example, the usual buy-in for $2–$5 No Limit is a rack of red ($500). To play in that game, you should have a $25,000 bankroll; losing 1/50 of your total available funds, while upsetting, won't destroy you. Some of the more conservative seasoned poker players take that philosophy one step further—they go by the 100-1 Rule. It all just depends on your monthly or annual earnings, your financial and personal obligations, your style of living, and, most important, the amount of money you feel comfortable losing.

We all want to believe we're invincible, especially at the poker table, but if you've played long enough to experience a bad beat—and chances are if you've played just once, you have—you'll know that anything can happen at any given time. By definition, that bad beat will anger and annoy you and leave you scratching your head in disbelief. But if it leaves you penniless and destitute, that's a bell that can't be unrung.

# 6 YOU NEVER GET A SECOND CHANCE TO MAKE A FIRST IMPRESSION

From the moment you sit down at the poker table, you're being watched, even if you're not aware of it. I'm not talking about the casino security's "eye-in-the-sky"—I'm talking about your opponents. After all, those sunglasses many poker players wear aren't being used just to mask their tells—they want to hide the direction in which they're looking. Constantly sizing one another up, players are forever scanning the table for a read on their adversaries' poker acumen and abilities. Cards aside, it's how those cards are played that will determine the difference between a winning session and a losing one. With that understanding in mind, it's paramount that you understand the first few hands you play—and the way you play them—will speak volumes about the type of player you are. Or, perhaps more important, the type of player you want your opponents to think you are.

Consider the movie *White Men Can't Jump*, starring Woody Harrelson and Wesley Snipes. When we first meet Harrelson's character (Billy Hoyle) down on the outdoor basketball courts in Venice, California, where a great deal of hustling takes place, he's acting like a total rube—a wannabe hoopster with little to no skills whatsoever. But after his "target audience" falls for the ploy and books the bet, the true nature of his character—a highly skilled player that can ball with the best of them—is revealed, and he goes on to win the wager easily.

Now apply that logic to the poker realm. Choose the image you want to convey and use that persona to your advantage. For example, if you are extremely selective early on in the session, playing sparingly with just a hand every now and then, and reveal solid starting hands (high pocket pairs, aces with big face cards), whenever there's a showdown, you will undoubtedly be pegged as a rock (a tight player) and will receive some modicum of respect, a label that should help you down the road if and when you decide to bluff someone off a pot. Unless they have an absolute monster, they will in all likelihood give you credit for your previous solid play and get out of your way.

Conversely, if you play a lot of hands right out of the gate, contest a lot of pots, and show a wider range of hands, you will be seen as a loose player, capable of having any two cards at any given time. While this image can work to your advantage if you're trying to trap a player by letting him think you are weak and simply calling him all the way down, it can also backfire if you try to bluff an opponent and he elects to make the call with a weak hand, but one that is still stronger than yours. In most cases, a looser style of play requires you to not only pick your spots more carefully but also use caution selecting the players you tangle with.

Table demeanor is also a major aspect of poker. Slow and steady, wild and crazy, passive-aggressive, or a combination of two styles—there's no right way or wrong way to play. And you can choose to embody any style at any given moment or session. In fact, some players will alter their playing style solely based on the other players at the table (often referred to as switching gears). It all boils down to finding a methodology that you are not only comfortable with but that also proves effective under the circumstances.

# 7 A CHANGE IN ATTITUDE IS BETTER THAN A CHANGE OF LATITUDE

**O**ftentimes, poker players who are experiencing a bad day at the table will switch seats, hoping to improve their luck in a different location. While it is true that luck does play a large role in the game of poker, more often than not the issue lies with the player, not the seat.

First, let's explore the concept of luck. Barring any shamanic activities, voodoo rituals, or Harry Potter–inspired spells, every poker player stands the same chance of getting lucky (or unlucky) as the next. Unless you have a black cloud following you around on a perpetual basis, or have done something in a past life to get the short end of the karma stick in this one, your individual luck factor is no different from anyone else's. However, for the vast majority of players, it's much easier to lay blame on external forces than to assume responsibility. And therein lies the difference between players who will forever be at the mercy of good and bad fortune and those who take the necessary strides to improve their poker skills and directly influence their results.

It goes without saying that some days you're the dog and some days you're the hydrant. It's the nature of the beast. Obviously, this applies to both life in general and to poker. Cards being what they are, in some sessions it will seem like a lucky horseshoe has been fused to your body, and the deck will deal you good cards repeatedly. Other sessions will be the polar opposite—you'll constantly come up second best with hands you simply cannot get away from. Scenarios such as these befall all poker players from time to time. Play long enough and sooner or later it will happen to you—if it hasn't already. But for all those other occasions, sessions when your luck is no better or no worse than your opponents, you owe it to yourself to make an accurate and honest assessment of your play, especially if you're losing.

Take a break from the action. Sit out a round or two and replay all of your losing hands in your head. Could you have done anything differently to change the result? Could you have been more aggressive? Or were you too aggressive? Did you miss a tell from your opponent, an obvious sign that gave away the strength of his hand? Or perhaps the problem lies even deeper; maybe you shouldn't have been in that hand to begin with. Or even deeper than that—maybe your mind is elsewhere and you shouldn't be playing cards at all that day.

By analyzing losing hands—hands where an opponent didn't have the stone-cold mortal lock (i.e., the nuts; the best possible hand), where he wouldn't have folded no matter what course of action you attempted—you should be able to spot flaws in your game. Identifying, isolating, and, ultimately, eliminating these flaws will put you on the path to playing perfect poker—if there is such a thing—and dramatically increase your chances of winning.

But it all starts with being honest—honest about your abilities, honest about your intentions, and honest about your emotional state. By changing your attitude instead of your latitude, you can quickly dispatch your greatest enemy at the poker table (your ego) and move on to battling your real adversaries (the other players) with an open mind.

# 8 YOUR CARDS ARE IMPORTANT—BUT SO ARE YOUR OPPONENT'S CARDS

It goes without saying that your cards are important. But it's imperative that you remember your opponents have cards as well. Too many players get tunnel vision when it comes to their own hand, both in its starting strength and in the best hand it can ultimately make after the flop, turn, and, most important, the river. Yes, pocket kings and pocket aces are the two best starting hands in poker. However, starting strength aside, one pair—even the biggest of pairs—is often not enough to rake a pot, depending on what the board is displaying. Yet many players simply refuse to let their hands go, even when it's brutally obvious they are beat—and beat soundly.

First, take into consideration how the pre-flop betting went down. If you've raised with a strong hand and gotten called in numerous spots, unless you're playing with a bunch of donkeys that regularly enjoy blowing off their chips, chances are at least one of them actually has a decent hand, maybe even a hand that's better than yours. Just because you don't get re-raised before the flop doesn't mean you're ahead. But once again, many players believe a show of weakness (such as a mere call to their raise) means they are leading going in.

After the flop, take a moment to study the board and see what's out there. Furthermore, look at what could potentially be out there. Are there straight draws? Flush draws? Both? Is the board paired (meaning someone could have flopped a full house)? Think of the hands you routinely play and whether those cards could result in any of the aforementioned draws. Remember, every hand has a plethora of possibilities, and the more players in the hand, the more possibilities there are. Don't just fixate on what you have or what you can make under a best-case scenario—try to envision what your opponents may be holding, or what they could be drawing to.

For example, let's say you have pocket aces, and your pre-flop raise yields two callers. First, you need to recognize the types of players you're up against. Are they tight or loose? Do they only call raises with high pocket pairs or big aces, or have they been known to take chances with lesser holdings in hopes of getting paid off? Now, look at the flop. If the cards are connected—such as 8-9-10—maybe with two of the same suit, not only could someone be drawing to a hand much stronger than a big pair (or a set if you happen to hit a third of your holding), they may also have already out-flopped you, in which case you are drawing extremely thin, if not completely dead.

Knowing when to stop throwing good money after bad (continuing to bet or call when the chances of your winning are slim to none) will play a key role in your development as a poker player and dramatically influence your ratio of winning sessions versus losing sessions.

Remember, unless you've got the stone-cold nuts—the best hand possible—a better hand is lurking out there ready to lock you in its unpleasant maw. Whether one of your opponents is actually holding a better hand still remains to be seen. But by allowing for that possibility, even remotely, you give yourself a much better chance of not only winning more but also losing less. And since poker often comes down to basic money management, folding, including the dumping of ferociously strong hands, is the same as winning. Sure, sometimes you're going to guess wrong and release a hand that would have won. But as the experts say, if you're not occasionally folding winners, you're not playing good poker.

# 9 POKER IS A MARATHON, NOT A SPRINT

By now I'm sure you've all heard the story of the tortoise and the hare. Fast out of the gate is certainly a force to be reckoned with, but if you're not going to make it to the finish, all that early speed is wasted. Such is the case with poker. And although this philosophy is primarily reserved for tournament play, it also holds water in cash games. Plain and simple, unless you can pace yourself and avoid the innumerable traps and pitfalls along the way, you'll never make it to the finish line (cashing in a tourney, or leaving a cash game a winner).

Some players act as though they are under time constraints, when in fact, they have all the time in the world. From playing almost every hand to being overly aggressive on every street, from the moment they sit down it's as though the bull has been turned loose in the china shop with the instructions to do as much damage as possible in the shortest period of time. Often, that's exactly what happens—the aggressive player is felted (busted) before the end of the first rotation, if he even lasts that long.

In other situations, players will immediately assume they have a solid read on their opponents, even if they are new to the game or the players in question, and try to establish their presence with authority by raising like a madman, using standard bully tactics to enforce their will. And although it's true to some extent that "fortune favors the bold," most of today's players simply won't tolerate those antics for long, especially from a newcomer to the table with an obvious kamikaze style.

The better approach is to ease into the game. Get to know your opponents, their tendencies, and their strengths and weaknesses. For the observant player, weaker players will quickly stand out like big red bull's-eyes on small white walls, and opportunities to take advantage of their deficiencies will definitely show themselves. In fact, the slower, more clandestine approach may actually create more opportunities to pillage and plunder rather than leave your opponents fearful and guarded, and therefore tighter-playing and less apt to make mistakes.

Many professional poker players are referred to as grinders for a reason. These astute card-smiths are more than willing to slog it out in the trenches, to dig in for the long haul, with the prescience that an intelligently cautious but willingly aggressive approach will yield big dividends whenever the right opportunity presents itself.

When you fill a bathtub with hot water, jumping in immediately after it's been filled is a rather foolish undertaking. If such a course of action results in your feeling scalded, you're not going to enjoy the bath. But if you first slip in a toe, then your foot, then your whole leg, and then climb in, you're going to enjoy that soothing soak for quite some time. And speaking of soaking, the object is to soak your opponents, not get soaked yourself.

# 10 THEY'RE SHOWING YOU NOTHING, BUT TELLING YOU EVERYTHING

Just because a poker player's cards are hidden from view doesn't mean you can't decipher what they are—or at the very least make an educated guess. By spotting tells (a visible change in a poker player's behavior or demeanor), you should be able to glean some insight as to their holding and, in turn, their hand's strength or weakness in comparison with your own.

The game of poker is as much about trickery and deception as it is about percentages and statistics. Customarily, only the most stoic and seasoned of cardsharps are able to maintain a steely exterior throughout the course of a poker session, thereby revealing nothing (or at least precious little) to their opponents. However, most players don't fall into this category. Sooner or later they will let their guard down, the result of which will be an unintentional tip-off that a pair of sunglasses or a tightly drawn hood (a la "the Unabomber") cannot conceal. But before you can take advantage of this valuable information, you first have to discover it.

One of the best times to pick up a tell is on the flop. Instead of looking at the board when the dealer reveals the first three cards, look at your opponents' faces. The cards aren't going anywhere—they'll be there when you need them. But upon that initial reveal, when most seated players are anxious to see what fate has in store for them, a momentary flicker of elation or disgust can go a long way toward pulling the pot in your direction. Naturally, this same scenario will unfold on the turn and on the river. Just be careful not to take a bite of that tasty-looking apple on the first pass. That is, observe your fellow competitors for a round or two before trusting that what you are witnessing is the real McCoy. Remember: trickery and deception. If your opponents are aware they are being watched—and most are, to some degree—they may try to feign jubilation or repulsion in an effort to throw you off or trap you. But if your opponents continually exhibit the same mannerisms, or some semblance thereof, chances are you've identified their tell and can now exploit it at your earliest opportunity.

But tells come in many forms, far beyond that of mere expressions and facial tics. Uncontrolled outbursts, posture shifts, shaking or wringing hands, sweating palms and brows, goose bumps, quivering lips, cottonmouth, crossing legs and tapping feet (you'd be amazed by what happens below the table), hair standing on end (I've seen this happen a number of times)—some of the best poker players on the planet occasionally fall victim to their own dead giveaways, no matter how hard they try to conceal them. In fact, in some situations, the more strenuously a person tries to hide their tell, the more obvious what that tell actually is.

Once you've spotted a tell, it is vital you keep the discovery under wraps. In *Rounders,* when Mike McDermott (Matt Damon) discovered the tell of Teddy KGB (John Malkovich)—the separating and eating, or not eating, of an Oreo cookie—he made a point of saying something about it, strictly to rile Teddy—to put him on tilt—not to mention clue the audience in as to what was happening. But in real life, protecting that knowledge—best done by keeping this information to yourself, along with taking your time before acting—will go a long way toward keeping your opponent in the dark about his inadvertent reveal. After all, you're not a medic. You don't want to cure anyone of their poker ills.

# 11 PEER PRESSURE IS FOR WIMPS

Let's get something straight—the poker table is not an extension of high school. Poker isn't about "in crowds" and circles of friends. And it certainly isn't about showing off or looking cool. I'm amazed whenever I see a poker player allow himself to be peer-pressured into making a call or a fold.

You have to be able to think for yourself at the poker table. Like boxing or mixed–martial arts, poker is, for the most part, a solo endeavor—just you against the world. Whether you're in the ring or out on the felt, you alone are responsible for your victory or defeat.

Going in, it's a given that psychological warfare will be a part of the game. Your opponents will say just about anything to goad you into doing whatever they want—or

need—you to do. The best example of this would have to
be during the 2006 World Series of Poker's $10,000 buy-in
main event, where former Hollywood talent agent and man-
ager Jamie Gold used a wide array of verbal ploys to run
over the tables en route to his $12 million first-place finish.
Start to finish, Gold had his opponents so mentally discom-
bobulated courtesy of his oral haranguing, he could have
told them he was Paul Bunyan and they would have offered
to babysit Babe, his trusty blue ox.

It's not Gold's skill that was surprising in this scenario—his gift of gab is well known in poker circles. It's that
his opponents gave his impromptu speeches credence—and
continually, no less. Had any or all of them elected to tune
him out and focus on what they knew to be real, to rely on
information they had observed themselves instead of the
"opinions" being heaped upon them, the outcome of that
event would probably have been decidedly different.

But the 2006 WSOP was not the first time this type of
peer pressuring took place; it happens to some degree at
virtually every poker session on the planet. However, this
was the first time it had happened on such a grand scale,
captured on video for all to see. It all boils down to a fear
of being shown up or embarrassed—the poker equivalent
of having your pants pulled down. It's why successfully car-
rying out a huge bluff and then showing the victim and the
rest of the table the cards that beat him can often result in
the bluffee going on tilt (a reckless poker binge that often
leads to going broke).

Succeeding in poker means checking your ego at the card room's door. You must completely close yourself off to even the slightest consideration of what anyone else—especially the other players at your table—may think about your ability or style of play. Never make a call or a fold because you're afraid of the reactions that showing or folding your hand may elicit. Steel your nerves and chalk whatever happens up to the information you had going into the situation, and the way you processed it. Sometimes, you're going to get it wrong and, yes, you may even feel a bit foolish afterward. But when you get it right, I promise you, your satisfaction will more than make up for the times you got it wrong.

# 12 RAGS TO RICHES

**B**eauty is in the eye of the beholder. This expression is especially true in poker. For example, although pocket aces or pocket kings—the theoretical and statistical best starting hands in Texas Hold'em—are looked upon as the next best thing since sliced bread by many a poker player, there is an entirely different contingent of players who prefer to do battle with far less strong and otherwise "invisible" hands.

One reason for such a tactic is that strong starting hands, such as the high pocket pairs, are harder to get away from (harder to fold), which can often spell disaster. But so-called ugly cards (smallish one-gappers, suited connectors, and the like) are not only easy to fold if the board isn't cooperative, but, if played creatively, can result in the winning of monster pots, mainly because those who fall victim will never see it coming.

Another reason playing rags ("trash cards") can be a viable alternative to playing stronger hands concerns the old poker adage: "Win a little pot or lose a big one," which is often the case with powerful pre-flop holdings. Considering that most players holding AA, KK, or similar strong starting hands will raise before the flop in an effort to "thin the herd"—ideally, they want to be in a heads-up scenario, where they are an overwhelming statistical favorite to any other holding—that raise will oftentimes chase away most, if not all, of the competition and, subsequently, the action. However, if the amount of the raise is too small or if the action is simply limped and not raised, thus bringing many callers into the fray, a nightmare situation is likely to develop. With multiple players in the hand, all of whom got in "on the cheap," the correct odds to pursue their draws are probably in place. And when you consider the perceived payoff that may result if they hit their hand, you'll likely need a brick of C4 and a detonator to get them to fold. With that in mind, making big money from a big hand often requires another big hand to pay you off.

Now, considering that you will only be dealt pocket aces once every 220 hands (expanded to once every 54 hands for any pair of face cards—AA, KK, QQ, JJ), simply waiting around for big hands to come your way may be a foolish and boring endeavor. Furthermore, if you do decide to play the waiting game, as many rocks (overly tight players) do, the strength of your holding will be obvious, and you'll be lucky to get any action at all.

Thus, the cards you will be getting in abundance—cards many players view as worthless or unplayable—can play a key role in your success. That's not to say you should play them all—you'll go broke in short order if you choose that route—but by picking your spots and taking advantage of situations and players that may be susceptible to a "rags-to-riches" strategy, you will add a whole new dimension to your game and become a feared and respected player, one who is capable of turning over any two cards at any given time. Remember, if they can't figure you out, they can't beat you.

Finally, there's the favorite hand aspect to consider. Yes, we all like pocket aces and pocket kings. Who doesn't? But some players have a favorite hand that, despite its relatively weak statistical value (such as jack-4, king-6, or Doyle Brunson's famous 10-2), the enormous confidence they have in it allows them to play it well and potentially become a winner. To that end, confidence should never be underestimated in any endeavor, especially poker, where belief and self-assurance can easily trump luck or skill.

# 13 TRUST YOUR GUT

According to early-twentieth-century politician Michael Burke, "Good instincts usually tell you what to do before your head has figured it out." Applying this sentiment to the game of poker, winning players know when to take pot odds, fold equity, and deal with the plethora of other poker-related statistics they've committed to memory ad nauseam and throw them right out the window.

Poker, like life, boils down to survival of the fittest. And oftentimes, survival depends less on logic and more on that little voice inside your head. While kicking logic to the curb may not seem like the wisest course of action, instinct, in general, has nothing to do with what's smart or dumb. Instinct, by definition, has everything to do with tapping into your primitive nature, the leftover remnant from a time when Man's "fight-or-flight" mechanism was relied upon daily.

I'm not talking about reading chicken innards or tea leaves or rubbing a crystal ball, although there are some scientists who believe instinctual decisions do involve a modicum of clairvoyance. I'm suggesting that learning to trust your gut can only come from within, without benefit of ritual adornments, apothecary potions, or outside assistance other than information that's already been gleaned the old-fashioned way: through simple observation.

For example, you're just a few hours into a poker session when you've observed your opponents in a variety of situations. You've seen them bluff and trap, check and raise, call and fold. Ultimately, you've seen them win and lose and, with each new victory or loss, have undoubtedly witnessed myriad mood changes and facial expressions, even some so minor that only your subconscious mind took note. Throughout it all, your brain has filed this information away like a biomatter supercomputer. Of course, there are no obvious files for all this knowledge—it is simply stored data, to be recalled in a nanosecond when a decision is required.

Now, factor in all that you have learned—even the information that doesn't appear obvious or relevant. A situation will arise that calls for a definitive course of action—one of those intersections where there are a number of ways to go, but just as it is with life, you can choose only one. In most cases, one of those decisions (such as a call or a fold) is the right decision, a decision that will reward you greatly. And if that's true, that means at least one decision is the wrong decision, a decision that will produce a less-than-stellar (if not worse) result.

Those are the trying times, the crux of it all when you not only have to listen to your gut but also act upon what your little voice is telling you. Whether you decipher this as a read of an opponent, a read of a situation, or simply chalk it up as an anomaly for which there is no legitimate explanation other than it seemed like the right thing to do at the time, learning to trust your gut is one of the most valuable tools a poker player can rely upon. In fact, at times, it just may be the only one.

# 14 THERE'S SAFETY IN NUMBERS

**Y**ou needn't be an MIT-educated math whiz with an understanding of rocket science–like computations to be a successful poker player. However, knowing the basic odds and statistics associated with key elements of the game will not only make you a better player but will also go a long way toward making you a winning player. Some of the most common and helpful statistics follow.

## Starting hands

In Texas Hold'em, there are exactly 1,326 possible starting hands for any given player. At a 10-handed table, that amounts to more than 622 quintillion possible hand combinations in play.

## Individual odds of being dealt

| | |
|---|---:|
| AK suited (or any two specific suited cards) | 331:1 |
| AA (or any specific pair) | 220:1 |
| AK (or any two specific non-suited cards) | 81.9:1 |
| AA, KK, QQ, or JJ | 54.3:1 |
| Suited connectors | 24.5:1 |
| Pocket pair | 16:1 |
| Suited cards | 3.25:1 |

## Odds of flopping certain hands

### With two unpaired cards

| | |
|---|---:|
| One pair | 2.7:1 |
| Two pair | 48.5:1 |
| Trips | 73.2:1 |
| Full house | 1,087.1:1 |
| Quads | 9,799:1 |

### With a pocket pair

| | |
|---|---:|
| Two pair | 5.2:1 |
| Set | 8.3:1 |
| Full house | 135.1:1 |
| Quads | 407.2:1 |

### With two suited cards

| | |
|---|---:|
| Backdoor flush draw | 1.4:1 |
| Flush draw | 8.1:1 |

| Making flush by the river | 14.6:1 |
|---|---|
| Flush | 117.8:1 |

*With connectors*

| Open-ended straight draw | 9.4:1 |
|---|---|
| Straight | 76.5:1 |

*With suited connectors*

| Straight or flush draw | 4.2:1 |
|---|---|
| Flush draw | 8.1:1 |
| Straight flush | 72,192:1 |
| Royal flush | 649,739:1 |

*Calculating "outs" and pot odds*

Outs—cards that will enable a player to make his hand—can be calculated reasonably quickly in this manner:

• Divide the number of cards unseen by the number of "outs."

• Subtract one.

• Now, to tell if you are getting the proper odds for your call, there needs to be at least an equal number of bets in the pot to the number of outs you have. Example: You are dealt two suited cards. The flop contains two more cards of that suit, meaning you have nine outs remaining to make your flush on the very next card. Forty-seven (unseen cards) divided by 9 ("outs") equals 5.2; 5.2 minus one equals 4.2. Thus, unless there are at least 4.2 bets in the pot, you should fold.

*Outs for improving a hand*

| | |
|---|---|
| Pair to a set | 2 outs |
| Two pair to a full house | 4 outs |
| Inside (gutshot) straight to a straight | 4 outs |
| Open-ended straight to a straight | 8 outs |
| Four-flush to a flush | 9 outs |
| Open-ended straight flush draw | |
| (for straight, flush, or straight flush) | 15 outs |

These are just a smattering of the odds a poker player faces on each hand. If you are truly serious about the game and have a genuine desire to improve, spend some time memorizing the various tables. Know your odds and percentages or, at the very least, how to calculate them. Some casinos and card rooms even allow you to keep odds tables with you while you play, although if you're trying to avoid being saddled with the novice label, you're much better off learning them rather than relying on tableside charts and graphs.

# 15 KNOW WHEN TO SAY "WHEN"

Every poker session must come to an end at some point. Knowing exactly when that point has been reached is key. For some, it's not until they've been busted to the felt and their ATM cards have all reached their limit. For others, it's after many hours of play, when their eyes can no longer remain open without benefit of stimulants, Velcro, or Krazy Glue. However, smart poker players, those who truly understand the nature of the game and the swings therein, will call it quits long before either of those extremes have come to pass.

Let's start with the positive. There are times when everything is going your way: the deck's hitting you in the head, your reads are spot-on, your opponents' reads are way off, and you just keep on raking pot after pot after pot. At times like these, walking away is exceedingly difficult. Nobody wants to stop in the midst of a heater (hot streak). But that's when the immortal words of Bud Fox (Charlie Sheen) to Gordon Gecko (Michael Douglas) in *Wall Street* should be reverberating in your ears. Bud said: "Tell me, Gordon, when does it all end? How many yachts can you waterski behind? How much is enough?"

Although we all remember Gecko's "greed is good" mantra, sooner or later, what goes up must come down. Rather than turn a great session into an okay session, or a good session into a bad session, resign yourself to the fact that you've had an amazing run, and now it's time to get out while the getting's good. In other words, don't leave the cozy comfort of the ski lodge to go back out for one last run. That last run, especially if the ski slope is a No Limit Hold'em table, could spell doom. Remember, even the most powdery of slopes still have ice and trees on them.

Before you start the day, set a win limit, or at the very least, a time limit. And make a promise to yourself to honor that number. For example, if your win limit is five times your original buy-in, have the willpower to rack up, stand up, and leave up. Even if that number takes only one or two hands to achieve, take your windfall and don't walk—run—to the nearest exit. Consider the alternative if your newfound riches weren't the result of one or two hands but many hours of play. Now imagine if you lost all those winnings in one fell swoop. How long might it take you to get back to that point and, honestly, will you be in any condition—mentally or physically—to try to regain it?

On the flip side, there's the ugly but very real possibility of losing sessions, scenarios no poker player wants to contemplate before sitting down to play. But there are some days, no matter what you do, when the Poker Gods have already elected you the designated loser, and fortune will simply not be in your cards, figuratively and literally. For those occasions—which I hope are few and far between—you must have the prescience to limit your losses by setting a loss limit. Whether it's three full buy-ins or three pots in a row or simply a time limit whereby if you're down, you're gone, once again, you need the willpower to call it a night.

In *Dirty Harry,* Inspector "Dirty" Harry Callahan (Clint Eastwood) said, "A man's got to know his limitations." If you can somehow manage to put your ego aside and accept defeat (many poker players have an exceedingly difficult time in this endeavor), with the attitude that "tomorrow is another day," you are well on your way to 24/7 ownership of a winning mindset and, ultimately, becoming the kind of poker player that others will fear.

# 16 A FOOL AND HIS MONEY ARE SOON PARTED

**W**inning at poker is no easy task. Even when your mind and body are in perfect harmony, both performing at their optimum capacities, cards and luck aside, achieving victory at the poker table is still a bone to be chewed. That being said, the worst thing you could possibly do is sit down to play when your faculties are in any way impaired, or if your mind is even slightly elsewhere.

To best illustrate this point, swing by your favorite poker room late one Friday or Saturday night (or early Saturday or Sunday morning) and do a recon of the players in attendance. It won't take long to spot the fresh arrivals—there will be a certain bounce in their step, even when seated—and it definitely won't take long to spot the players who have been there overnight. Now, hover close and watch the game, focusing not on the cards or the action but on the antics and play of the overnighters. Chances are, you'll be shocked by what you witness. Sloppy would be the term I'd use to describe it, although that might be a tad too respectful. But from their overall lethargy and downright foolish play, I'm certain you'll understand the point I'm driving home.

And speaking of driving, playing poker when your head is clouded or your sensibilities are even modestly diluted is akin to operating a motor vehicle while under the influence. Sooner or later something bad is going to happen. You might avoid disaster the first time you try it, but keep on rolling the dice and the odds will be mounting against you with each new attempt. And when that accident comes to fruition (and believe me, it will), there won't be an insurance agency to repair the damage. In fact, just the use of the word "accident" is misleading in both scenarios. Accidents are unfortunate happenings that occur without planning or deliberate intent. But willingly and knowingly placing yourself in a bad situation (anything requiring serious concentration or deep thought while impaired qualifies) hardly constitutes an accident.

Some of the greatest names in poker have had, shall we say, issues that took them away from their A-games; in many cases, far, far away. Without naming names, there's enough published and televised documentation out there, including Q & A's and interviews with the players, that describe in detail some of their bone-headed, alcohol-induced, drug-

or stress-induced poker antics and the less-than-enviable results.

When money is on the line—and let's face it, that's the primary reason most people play poker—you want to do everything in your power to stack the odds in your favor, even if it's just enough to tip the scales. Doing anything counterproductive to that end is pointless. Sitting down at a poker table when you're not prepared or not able to actually focus on the game and your opponents is the worst thing you can do.

# 17 DON'T ALLOW EGO TO TAKE THE PLACE OF LOGIC

News flash: bad beats happen. Play poker long enough, and sooner or later you're going to get snapped off on a monster pot when you're way ahead and the odds are solidly in your favor. If you are uncomfortable with that eventuality, I strongly urge you to take up chess or checkers or backgammon or Monopoly and quit playing poker immediately. But accepting that you will indeed be the victim of misfortune somewhere down the poker road is only half the equation—it's how you respond to that unfortunate but eventual circumstance that will ultimately determine your card-playing fate.

Far too often I see a player get donked upon, only to embark on an all-out revenge binge against the player (or players) who walloped him. From calling out of position, to calling raises with substandard hands, to raising just for the sake of raising, to trying to isolate the offending player or players solely for payback, the runaway train is obvious to everyone at the table—everyone except the runaway train himself. But in those instances, the desire for retribution undoubtedly exceeds all sense of intelligent play; it's a tunnel-vision scenario of the worst kind, most likely leading to the sooner-than-later depletion of an entire chip stack.

If you're not the kind of player who can simply accept the unplanned defeat, you should immediately get up from the table, or leave the card room or casino completely, and not return until you are level-headed and even-keeled enough to play rationally and within your own limits and abilities. Staying put, or coming back sooner than you're ready, will have only one result, and it certainly isn't a good one. Sure, you may get lucky and do unto those as they have previously done unto you, but unless you're trying for irony (don't be silly, you're trying to win), getting your money in bad isn't what poker or winning poker is all about.

They say that "revenge is a dish best served cold," which essentially means keen planning and complete emotional detachment will yield the greatest vengeance. From a poker standpoint, that is the quintessential way to get even with those who have needed to get lucky to beat you. Think about it: if they had to get lucky to win, that means you outplayed them right up to the point when your luck soured. But regardless of the circumstances that led up to the turn of the tides, you were ahead and they were behind. Even if it's fleeting, take some solace in that accomplishment. Wouldn't it be more satisfying to stick to your guns and beat them by playing good, smart poker? Not only will you recoup your losses (some, perhaps all, maybe even with interest) from a financial standpoint, you will have the added contentment of knowing you didn't fall into the "tilt trap," which is exactly what your nemesis, along with the rest of the table, will be hoping for.

# 18 REPUTATIONS ARE EARNED, NOT INHERITED

**P**oker players are, by nature, a rough-and-tumble lot. Regardless of age, gender, or social standing, the intestinal fortitude and mental toughness required to be a poker player—at any skill level—is off the charts. Thus, if you want the reputation of a rounder—a highly capable cardsharp—where other poker players respect and possibly fear you, you can't simply ask for it; you have to earn it. And that's only going to occur by proving to them beyond a shadow of a doubt that you're a force to be reckoned with.

The reputation of a skilled poker player, and the respect that comes with that label, can yield big dividends. It can aid in your ability to pull off bluffs. It can cause other players to give you a much greater leeway of hand strength. And it can cause players to think twice about raising you, thereby allowing you to pursue more draws on the cheap. But once again, if you think that a solid reputation and the attached measure of respect will come your way because you look like or act like a tough guy, you're in for a very rude awakening.

Image, while important, is not a substitute for skill—or lack thereof. In the beginning, an all-business, take-no-prisoners demeanor might get you a smattering of street credibility, but as soon as your opponents discover that you're all smoke and no fire, even the weakest of the bunch will descend upon you like a lion on a wounded gazelle. Barking dogs may be feared at the onset, but if they have no chompers to do any damage, even the wimpiest of cats will take them on sooner or later.

Now, on the flip side, even if you look like Joe Cupcake or come across as the most soft-hearted person in the room, if you exhibit cutthroat tendencies, make spot-on reads, show down quality hands, successfully trap opponents, and most of all, aren't afraid to take a beating every now and then in an effort to make a big score, chances are the other players at the table will have no choice but to proceed with caution when you're in a pot with them.

Keep in mind, however, that a formidable reputation and the associated respect simply cannot be earned in the immediacy; it's accrued over time, where you are judged by the totality of your play, not just by a few hands or rounds. Consistency is the key—and not just being a consistent winner, for bad luck (and bad beats) can befall anyone. It's consistent strong showings that will make other players step back and take notice, for accomplished players are not soon forgotten. In fact, a player who handles defeat well and bounces back with even greater tenacity is much scarier than a loose cannon with a penchant for bad beat–inspired retribution.

A reputation as a donkey is very easy to acquire. Just play like a fool and you'll have other players foaming at the mouth to get a seat at your table. Although this could potentially yield some good action in the beginning, chances are it will do more harm than good in the long run, as everyone will be putting you squarely in their crosshairs. And being singled out as an easy target is definitely not the reputation you want. Again, it may work out once in a while, but overall, you'll be sorry.

The moral, then, is to play your best poker all the time. If you know you're not up to the task on a specific occasion, or if you're thinking about having a goof session, get out of there and do something more productive with your time and energy. Remember, it can take a lifetime to earn a solid reputation, but only a fleeting moment to tear it apart.

# 19 IT'S NOT WHAT YOU HAVE, IT'S WHAT THEY THINK YOU HAVE

Missing your draw isn't the worst thing that can happen at a poker table, especially if your opponents aren't aware that your hand isn't worth navel lint. Getting your opponents to think you've got them beat, even if—and especially when—you don't, is a key aspect of becoming a consistently winning poker player. After all, you're not going to make your hand every time. In fact, you're not going to make it half of the time. It's these situations where the element of bluffing comes into play, and everything you've done at the poker table up to that point will play a huge role in how successful (or unsuccessful) your attempt will be.

First things first—you can't bluff all the time. Yes, you can certainly try, but eventually your tablemates will catch on and start calling you down—and keep calling you down until the cows come home. The saying "It only has to fail once" carries major weight in poker, especially in No Limit Texas Hold'em, as one poorly timed bluff can leave you busted or on the brink. A well-known poker champion once had desires of becoming the greatest bluffer in the history of poker. Unfortunately, he made this sentiment public, and wouldn't you know it, for nearly two years after his big WSOP win he not only failed to win a single event—even a small one—he didn't even cash, let alone reach a final table.

Therefore, bluffing can only work when your opponents truly believe you've got the goods. It's much easier for a tighter, more selective player to pull off such a move because his poker history consists of only solid play; he's not taking fliers or chasing odd draws and turning up "donkey cards" to rake pots. In all probability, this player has successfully bluffed before, only he was given so much respect that nobody called him down to see his hand—yet more proof that a solid reputation can pay dividends.

On the other side of the fence, a wild player known for his willingness to gamble and take chances—which includes pursuing draws till the very end (the river)—will be much easier to pick off. Even novice players can read a board and get a sense of when their opponents are drawing (for straights or flushes). And if that's their take on the situation and a blank card hits the river, even going all-in cannot erase your prior loosey-goosey action, and a call will likely result.

More than once I've watched insanely aggressive players push all-in on the river, only to get called by a player holding bottom pair. This often leads to a verbal tirade, the beaten player hurling derogatory poker terms like "fish" and "donkey" at the victor. But the reality is the failed bluffer has only himself to blame. His play was so obvious a blind man would have seen it, let alone another player with cash invested in the pot.

Finally, there's the semi-bluff. Even if you missed your draw, if you read your opponent for a miss as well, your bet will more than likely earn you the pot. Just be careful you don't give your opponent the opening to come back over the top, thereby preventing your call or re-raise and further compounding your fiscal injury.

If you pick your spots and your opponents carefully, you will be rewarded.

# 20 HEALTHY POKER EQUALS WINNING POKER

You seldom see top-shelf athletes in poor mental or physical shape. Although there are some exceptions, being of sound mind and body has definite advantages, especially when it comes to competition. And poker—cash games or tournaments—is definitely a form of competition. This doesn't mean you have to be a physical specimen to have success on the felt, but when you consider the mental acuity, patience, and stamina that poker requires, especially for marathon cash games and multiday tournaments, good health, both internally and externally, can give you a decided edge over your adversaries.

*Sleep.* I'm sure you know how haggard and lazy you feel when your sleep cycle has been disrupted. Trying to calculate odds and read opponents when your mind is in tip-top shape is hard enough, but to do it when you're run down and foggy is virtually impossible. Therefore, get plenty of rest, especially prior to your poker sessions. And if you know you're going to play for a long time, try to get in a few extra hours. Even if you're not actually sleeping, relaxing in calm and quiet surroundings can be hugely beneficial.

*Nutrition.* Despite the "back-of-the-bar" stigma that the game of poker is often associated with, your diet doesn't have to reflect all the fried finger foods and tasty but non-nutritious munchies taverns and saloons are famous for (fries, onion rings, chicken wings, nachos, et cetera). Think of your body like an engine; poor fuel choices will keep it running, but not at optimal levels. By keeping a balanced diet, ingesting all the necessary proteins, carbohydrates, and vitamins the body requires daily, you'll feel healthier and stronger. In turn, you will play better. Of course, it's important to apply this outlook on nutrition all the time, not just when you're playing poker.

*Hydration.* While there is no definitive answer as to the exact amount of water a person should ingest daily, the Mayo Clinic, one of the most respected health and wellness organizations in the world, advises eight 8-ounce glasses daily. Most poker players don't get anywhere near this amount, choosing instead to satiate their thirst with soft drinks, energy drinks, tea and coffee, or alcoholic beverages. Just because you're not sweating profusely doesn't mean you're not losing hydration. Make it a point to drink more water during your next session and watch how much better and more alert you feel, which in turn should help you concentrate more and ultimately play better poker.

*Exercise.* Although you don't have to become a gym rat or start running marathons, some form of exercise—even a short daily walk—will not only prolong your life, it will improve your overall well-being, including the time you spend at the poker table. Lately, it seems that many professional poker players—or at least those who play cards regularly—have completely abandoned their fitness regimens, instead devoting all their free time to the tables. News flash: the games aren't going anywhere. They will surely be there when you're done working out. Even if your path to some sort of fitness involves purchasing a dog simply to get in the habit of taking daily walks, do it. Animal shelters are full of adoptable mutts, and the ends will justify the means. Heck, get a new pup with your poker winnings and let the pooch return the favor by helping to extend your life.

# 21 THE EYES HAVE IT

The eyes are the windows to the soul," or so said famous psychoanalyst Harry Stack Sullivan. The hugely successful rock band the Eagles seemed to agree, as their hit song "Lying Eyes" suggested. And in poker parlance, the eyes are often the key to determining whether a player really has the goods or is just blowing smoke.

Although tells are revealed through many channels—body language, fluctuations in voice, talkativeness or silence, sweating, et cetera—reactive eye movements are often the initial giveaway. Trust me, the poker players you see wearing sunglasses aren't doing so because it's too bright in the card room.

Some players, novices and pros alike, are able to dilute or eliminate their macular disclosures and prefer to play poker sans tinted eyewear. However, for those players who cannot hide their "retinal emotions," the protection that darkened shields provide is invaluable. After all, telling lies at the poker table is a huge part of the game.

As you would expect, poker is far from the first medium that paid serious attention to visual cues. Law enforcement has been relying on the close examination of suspects' eye movements for ages. While some miscreants are overly creative with their alibis, oftentimes they have no control over the actions of their bodies, and the gig is up quickly no matter how convincing the tale they spew.

Notable poker strategists, among them Mike Caro ("The Mad Genius of Poker"), have devoted considerable time to this subject. And not long ago, FBI counterintelligence agent Joe Navarro, a specialist in nonverbal communications, hooked up with world-renowned poker professional Phil Hellmuth to produce a series of books, videos, and lectures on how to read players and spot tells.

Although it takes a considerable amount of training to be able to pick a liar out of a lineup 100 percent of the time, anything you can do to tip the scales in your favor—even slightly—can mean the difference between winning and losing. To that effect, at your next poker session, make it a point to watch your opponent's eyes each time the dealer reveals the flop, turn, and river. Sooner or later you are bound to discover something. And once you can identify a pattern, you will possess a significant advantage over that player for every hand to come. Even if your attempt at profiling is only somewhat accurate, the scrutiny alone may cause the subject to reveal even more to you—information that may have remained hidden had you not tried to read him in the first place. Remember, it's not the method that matters, just the results.

# 22 JABS CAN WIN A FIGHT JUST AS EASILY AS A KNOCKOUT PUNCH

**E**verybody loves a knockout. From a visual standpoint, they're exciting to watch. But a decision victory will put a check mark in the win column just the same. Sure, it might take a little longer, but the result is identical. The same concept applies to poker. Winning monster pots is certainly a thrilling endeavor and will go a long way toward pumping up your balance sheet. But winning a slew of smaller pots can result in an equally impressive tally. In fact, the yield can ultimately be greater since many players look upon small pots as being unworthy of contesting and are therefore quick to get out of the way, making them ripe for the taking.

Depending on your style of play and, even more important, the type of game you're in and the type of players you are battling against, in the early stages of the session you should be able to formulate some semblance of a plan—if you're thinking strategically, that is. Rather than just let the game develop—let the game come to them, so to speak—some players prefer to go into a poker session with a defined strategy: to attack many small pots or to concentrate on winning fewer larger ones. Of course, many other factors come into play—length of time you will be playing, risk versus reward mentality, and available bankroll are some of the more obvious.

Generally speaking, smaller pots constitute less risk, although a small pot can quickly turn into a large one, especially when playing No Limit. Conversely, larger pots, which almost always involve more individual exposure (family pots excluded, where many or all seated players are involved), obviously make for great stories; however, not all stories will have a happy ending—the game of poker and fairy tales share no bloodlines.

Although placing an emphasis on stealing blinds, targeting less aggressive players, and purposely keeping your betting to a bare minimum when pursuing draws may seem a bit tedious and humdrum, taking the "small-pot approach" can nevertheless amount to a hefty payday.

Tight players (a.k.a. rocks) are content to grind out their sessions, folding hand after hand after hand, including those that many looser players would strongly consider raising with, and joining the fray only when they are certain they are an odds-on favorite. Again, this may not seem the most colorful style—it's certainly a far cry from the "trap and re-trap" variant of poker that has become so popular on television—but if you watch disciplined players' antics closely, you'll notice they scoop far more pots than they lose.

From a cash-game standpoint, this may seem like an alien concept, far too regimental or significantly less fun than more off-the-cuff alternatives. But for beginning tournament players (who have not yet become accustomed to attacking often and early), where staying alive and slowly climbing the leader board is a necessity, slow and steady should keep you around much longer and, with a little luck, present more opportunities for a big score.

# 23 DON'T BE THE TABLE SHERIFF

Like the safety position on a football team's defensive squad, who is tasked with preventing any offensive player from getting past him, the role of the "table sheriff" in poker is to prevent anyone from stealing a pot without at least having to show his cards. From an informational standpoint, a table sheriff is an invaluable commodity at any poker game since no one will be able to consistently buy (win uncontested) pots. But from a money management standpoint, the table sheriff is the last thing you want to be.

How many times have you heard a poker player say, "I'll take one for the team" or "I'll keep you honest"? First, there are no teams at the poker table. It's dog-eat-dog, every man for himself. As for honesty, considering that the game is steeped in trickery and deception, decide for yourself whether that concept should apply. If someone wants to throw his own money or chips into the mix to potentially prevent another player from scoring a cheap victory, or to simply get a look at another player's cards, more power to them. But don't you be the fall guy. Once in a while won't hurt, but making a habit of it is foolish.

Personally, I liken table sheriffs to boat owners—it's much better to have a friend who owns a boat than to own one yourself, for the simple reason that boats—tons of fun initially—almost always turn out to be gaping holes in the water that you fill with money. Essentially, table sheriffs are the same thing. Yes, the service they provide at the onset of the game is important, but eventually the information the table sheriff is purchasing should be readily available to an astute player, even without the luxury of seeing the would-be thief's cards.

Oftentimes, players will get goaded into becoming the sheriff. For example, a player is heads-up and their opponent, who has been pushing the action the entire hand, has just made his final bet. Seeing the pondering player on the fence, the others at the table will—wrongfully—make a comment that is intended to bring about a call.

First, talking about a hand that you're not directly involved in is one of the great "no-no's" of poker. People have actually been shot over such an offense, although the more common result is a stern lecture from the floorman (in tournaments, it's almost always a penalty). But poker ethics aside, your actions at the table, especially when you're involved in a hand, should be yours alone. We've covered this before, but it is imperative you never allow anyone else, no matter your relationship or their skill level, to influence your decision when it comes to calling, raising, or folding.

And as for the table sheriff, post-hand you can thank him, congratulate him, heck, even buy him a drink or dinner, but never—and I mean never—try to emulate him. It's a title you don't want bestowed upon you under any circumstances.

# 24 TEST THE WATERS

In any poker hand, information is garnered by betting. Some players will argue that checking will also yield information, but I strongly disagree. Any information that passivity may provide will undoubtedly prove misleading in the long run.

Checking—declining to bet—is the same as playing the role of Switzerland during a major international crisis. By assuming a neutral position, not only do you not make your intentions known (not always a bad thing, depending on the scenario), but from a tactical standpoint, you also yank the door wide open for another player to assume control. And in most cases, each hand or pot—which I compare to individual battles or skirmishes rather than to the war—will be won by the first player to seize control of the action.

By betting—or raising if a bet has already been made—you immediately put an opponent to the test. Not only have you taken an aggressive posture, which may alone win the battle for you, you're now forcing your opponent to decide how far he is willing to go in pursuit of that hand. Even if you plan on folding to a re-raise—information that, unless he is clairvoyant, he obviously will not be privy to—your opponent can no longer just be a passive observer, a scenario that checking promotes.

Some players, especially those who have a very strong hand, prefer to check in early position in hopes of trapping their opponent down the road. Although this can be a worthwhile tactic if building a large pot is the intent, bad things can easily happen. First, a strong hand–early position check can be greeted by another check right behind it, thus adding no money to the pot. (The saying "A bird in the hand beats two in the bush" comes to mind.) Second, that free card could very well give your opponent the card he needed to beat you. Now, not only have you let him catch up (and for free), you probably still think you're ahead, in which case you're headed for a severe chip swing, and you're going to be on the wrong end.

The style employed by the vast majority of professional tournament players is a great example of betting for information. Seldom do you see them entering a pot pre-flop without a raise. Not only are they trying to assume control of the hand—regardless of their position—right then and there, they are trying to flush out any other strong hands, or at least get a sense of a player who will try to contest the pot. Plus, an early position bet—or a late-position raise—has the added bonus of conveying strength, even if the hand is softer than marshmallow fluff. This is why you often see a continuation bet—a follow-up bet from the previous street's aggressor (usually concerning a pre-flop raise and a bet on the flop) regardless of what the flop is—and that follow-through wager wins the pot. And though there is much more to poker than simply power and aggression, the term "fortune favors the bold" is marinated in truth, as is "the early bird gets the worm," both concepts that can be applied to this game.

In war, weapons are obviously the instruments of destruction. But those weapons cannot be properly employed without correct information—both for their usage and for the targets at which the attack is directed. Thus, information is the real key to victory.

# 25 POKER ISN'T A SCHOOLYARD FIGHT; SWING FIRST

The same advice trainers and cornermen give to boxers and mixed–martial artists applies to poker players as well. Simply put: swing first.

Poker is not a schoolyard showdown. The last time I checked, no player was ever sent to the principal's office for being the aggressor in a hand. In Texas Hold'em, especially No Limit, more often than not the first player to bet ends up winning the pot. Think about that from a real-world perspective. It's much harder to call a bet than it is to make a bet. Even if your opponent has nothing—and you know he has nothing—if you also have nothing, his nothing could easily be better than your nothing, so you can't possibly match his wager. Of course, you could go over the top and push all-in, but it takes a steely nerve to put all your cash or chips at risk with nothing, which is why most players avoid that play like the plague.

There is a famous story involving the late Stu Ungar, possibly the greatest No Limit Texas Hold'em player the game has ever known. Stu made a huge all-in call against a seasoned player, 1990 WSOP main-event champion Mansour Matloubi, with only 10-high. Again, this is the fearless, ferocious, and brilliant Stu Ungar; his rationale doesn't really apply to the rest of the poker world, as evidenced by the many televised poker tournaments and cash games on the airwaves that allow us to glimpse players' hole cards. Most of the time, the first player to swing at a pot takes it down.

Obviously, there are a great many factors that come into play when deciding whether to check or bet. But parsing it all down, if you're on the fence, sometimes it's better to simply throw caution to the wind and take a stab at it. For one, the odds are likely in your favor. Regardless of the pot size, one bet has to be smaller than the total amount already in the pot. And though this can be a predicament in a No Limit game—how much to bet is often the quandary—with a little thought on the matter, the right amount (an amount that other players would consider too great to risk if they are unsure about the strength of their hand) shouldn't be too difficult to figure. (Some seasoned pros swear by a 75-percent-of-the-pot bet, but again, it all depends on the situation.)

Second, even if you get raised, thus forcing you to fold, losing one bet in an effort to drag a pot containing many bets seems the smart play. Over time, if you multiply it out (lost bets versus pots won), the percentages will clearly favor the aggressor.

There is an old poker saying: "If you can't bet, you can't win." If you come across more sage advice, please, let me know. Until then, swing first.

# 26 TAKE BREAKS

**E**ven the greatest minds lose focus from time to time. Undue stress, heavy concentration, less-than-stellar nutrition, lack of sleep . . . there are many possible causes, and sometimes all of these can occur simultaneously during one session of poker.

For those who have never participated in a marathon cash game or a large, multi-table tournament, where intense concentration is required every step of the way—winning other people's money or chips while protecting your own is absolutely exhausting—take my word for it. But even a low-stakes, run-of-the-mill poker game can be taxing on the mind and body. By taking breaks every so often to recharge your batteries, you can gain a decisive edge on the competition (especially if they are not following a similar regimen) and assure yourself of playing your best poker every time.

Scientists and researchers could easily launch a field study to measure the benefits enjoyed by poker players who leave the table mid-game to get a breath of fresh air, enjoy a healthy meal in calm, quiet surroundings, or even take a cat nap, comparing and contrasting the results with data acquired from players who elect to remain seated and play without any interruptions. But it doesn't always require an experiment or a control group to understand the obvious.

Some poker pundits have compared playing poker to driving an automobile on an unfamiliar road during a rainstorm; there are many potential hazards to watch out for en route to your destination beyond all the basic details of operating a motor vehicle. Now, add great distance into the equation. For those of you who have experienced such a road trip, you'll no doubt remember the toll it took on you, mentally and physically. If you weren't totally spent and seriously famished at the end of your jaunt, I'd love to see a scan of your genome, as you've probably got a little superhero DNA lurking inside you. Granted, poker does not contain the same life-or-death complexities that driving in inclement weather on potentially hazardous road surfaces does— although some extreme high-stakes players could certainly mount an argument to the contrary—but the same general sentiment applies. In either case, you simply cannot let your guard down, not even for a second. That momentary lapse could spell doom, landing you in a situation from which it is nigh impossible to recover.

Besides providing you with much-needed rest, taking a break from the action will also allow you to consider objectively what has unfolded up to that point in the session. Whether it's an in-depth scrutiny of your opponents or a fair and honest assessment of your own play, stepping away and reflecting should yield an accurate analysis and, if you respect your findings, a crystal-clear picture of whether you should continue playing.

# 27 PLAY THE MAN, NOT THE CARDS

There are widely varying schools of thought on this topic of playing the man and not the cards, but it really depends on the individuals in the hand and the type of game they're embroiled in. However, if I had to choose definitively between the two—an all-or-nothing decision, per se—considering the nature of poker, where deceit and trickery are the very fabric of the game, I'd opt to play the man, not the cards. My reasoning is simple: though the cards will ultimately decide the winner (and that's only if a showdown is required), if you can sniff out weakness or trepidation in your opponent, the cards are largely unimportant.

This is where the whole skill versus luck debate takes over. And it should come as no surprise that in many states and municipalities, poker has been determined to be a game of skill, not luck, and is therefore not placed in the same category as bingo or the lottery when it comes to taxing your winnings. Thus, if skill is the primary factor, and assuming we all experience the same basic trends and swings in luck (both good and bad), playing the man, not the cards, makes far more sense.

From a tournament perspective, where the blinds are constantly rising and each round has a set time limit, failing to amass chips—in some cases quickly—will result in elimination. With what we know about the concept of luck, there are no guarantees you will get good cards. Truth is, you may not even be dealt any playable hands in the entire event. Sounds crazy, I know, but I've seen it happen many times. What then? Do you simply accept your fate and continue folding like an automaton, hoping to get lucky when your final chips go into the pot? Or do you take a more proactive approach to the game, grabbing the bull by the horns?

If you look at today's top tournament players—and most of the professional poker players, in general—the one common trait they all share is that they refuse to wait around for perfect hands. Unless you're of the mindset that every time a pro player raises before the flop he has a good starting hand—and if you really believe that, poker should not be your game of choice—it should be obvious that the pros are routinely playing their opponents, capitalizing on their weaknesses, and not playing the cards they have been dealt.

Your beginning rounds of cash games, or early tournament rounds where the blinds are small, should be used to assess the competition—a reconnaissance mission, if you will. Try to determine who the solid players are and who is less confident with their game. Get a sense of the players who will not be forced off a hand with a flamethrower and those who can be bullied with a dirty look, not to mention how far you can bully them. Once that information has been gleaned, I'd recommend utilizing a numerical ranking system based on the total number of players at the table—for example, if there are nine players, 1 for the alpha player and 9 for the weakest. Then, mentally dole out the numbers, being honest with your own placement. After the rankings are assigned, focus your attention on the players you believe are weaker than you and try to isolate and engage them in pots whenever possible, regardless of the cards in your hand or on the board.

In terms of the showdown, obviously the fewer hands you have to show, the better. The less information you reveal to your opponents, the harder it will be for them to know when you're gaming them and when you actually have a monster. To that effect, I like to show a big hand every now and then, even if I didn't get called, just to establish a solid reputation. Conversely, I never show a bluff; I don't ever want my opponents thinking I'd resort to trickery to win a pot. It might plant a seed in their heads that would be impossible to get rid of.

I have heard incredible stories of players who cut blistering swaths through tournament fields without ever having to show down their cards until they reached the final table.

Although that scenario is certainly possible, I wouldn't count on it. Thus, timing will play an important role in your "man versus cards" strategy. If you target the right players and pick the right spots, there is no end to the rewards you can reap. Of course, if you are not clever with your exploits, serious peril awaits.

lar note, I'm acquainted with an extremely competent golf hustler who makes it a point to look like he doesn't belong out on the links—everything from mismatched equipment to thrift-shop gear. He even tanks a few shots on the practice range before the round to fully sell the image he's peddling. And let me tell you, more times than not he winds up getting a juicy match and a bunch of strokes to boot. Last I checked, his ratio of victories to defeats was nearly six to one.

Other players subscribe to the "comfort-is-key" theory: it doesn't matter what they wear or how they look so long as they are relaxed and comfortable. If they could bring a BarcaLounger to the game with them, I'm sure they'd do it. Soft, loose-fitting clothing is the customary wardrobe, with sweat suits and hoodies in high demand. I also know a player who brings a backpack with him to the table whenever he plays, swapping out his shoes for plush slippers right before beginning a session.

Finally, there are poker players who, like many professional athletes, are highly superstitious. Firmly entrenched in the "If it ain't broke, don't fix it" camp, if they have a winning session while wearing a specific wardrobe, chances are you will see them wearing the same ensemble until their luck changes. I heard tales of one player who wore the same clothing, right down to his underwear and socks, for eleven days straight. On the twelfth day, every player who was unfortunate enough to be placed in a seat neighboring his asked (or begged) to be moved. Fortunately for the other players, Mr. Superstitious lost that session—badly, from what I heard—and was in clean duds the following day, much to everyone's delight.

Of course, if you're primarily an Internet player, pajamas, bathrobes—heck, even poker in your birthday suit is doable and nobody can tell you otherwise.

Bottom line: find a look that works for you and don't veer away from it, regardless of the feedback.

# 29 BEWARE THE PLAYER WHO HAS NOTHING TO LOSE

**C**lueless, reckless, unafraid or uncaring of the outcome— we've all seen the kamikaze poker player before. Whether he's drunk, stupid, or an equal measure of both is irrelevant. All that matters is he's going to rain on someone's parade in a major way. Players like this need to be avoided like the plague.

Some players actually enjoy having a chip-burner in their game in the hopes of catching him in a big pot. While there's a definite upside—his chips will always be in play no matter what cards he's holding—the downside is that all the poker skill in the world won't do you any good. Unhinged players don't know when they're beat. They don't care about pot odds—I'd be shocked if they even understood the concept—or drawing percentages or anything else even remotely statistical or mathematical in nature. In fact, it's highly doubtful they ever even consider what another player might be holding or what hand that player can make to beat them. No, the only thing they care about is the two cards in their hands and the ones on the felt. That's it. So while it's certainly possible that a crazy player will donk off all his chips to you in a classic display of anti-poker, Murphy's Law will undoubtedly say otherwise. As a result, the monster hand you think you're going to win, putting you well into the black, will have an unanticipated ending. Namely, you'll flip over your two beautiful cards and the maniac in question will smile and turn over the two ugliest cards in the deck. Long story short, he'll still be stacking your chips long after you've managed to scrape your lower jaw off the table.

When you eventually encounter this type of player—it's not a question of if but when—don't allow your ego to override your intelligence. Too many players think their poker prowess can combat and ultimately defeat pure insanity. Here's a news flash for you: it can't. Even if you win a few of the smaller battles, one big hand is all it takes for the war to be decided.

Case in point: a seasoned rounder played mid-level stakes for months, grinding away at session after session to build up a bankroll large enough to take a shot at one of the bigger games that his favorite card room offered—$25/$50 No Limit Hold'em. Eventually he had the necessary starting stake, and he took his seat. Unfortunately, he chose a day when the craziest player in the house decided to play a game far smaller than the nosebleed stakes he usually played. The seasoned rounder played brilliant, disciplined poker for hours, folding when he wasn't sure, pouncing when he was. His chip stack grew steadily, soon reflecting a near 400 percent profit. And that's when he picked up a monster hand—you guessed it, pocket rockets—and found himself heads-up with the kamikaze after a hefty pre-flop raise. The flop, turn, and river played out—a mixture of what looked to be useless cards considering the pre-flop raise—and all the money went in. The seasoned rounder triumphantly revealed his cards and reached for the gargantuan pot, ready to rake it in. With a shrug, the goofball turned over his two trolls—unsuited multi-gappers—face-up, and that was that. The seasoned rounder just skulked away from the table, busted all the way back down to the smallest game in the joint.

The moral of the story: if you find yourself at a poker table with one of those aforementioned crazy players, do yourself a favor and put your name back on the board ASAP!

# 30 TAKE NOTES ON YOUR OPPONENTS

**A**ny spy worth his trench coat will confirm wholeheartedly that information is everything. The more you know about a person or a situation, the better you'll be able to control the action, regardless of what it is you are trying to accomplish.

Throughout the world, the rules regarding "additional materials" at the poker table are virtually the same: provided the "materials" are not interfering with the game, they are allowed to be present. And if you've played poker in any brick-and-mortar card room, be it a tournament or a cash game, chances are you've noticed players reading magazines, novels, newspapers, or some other form of printed material. I've even seen players reading poker "how-to" books, along with specialized index cards used for calculating odds or draw percentages. So if you're allowed to read at the table, it goes without saying that writing at the table is also condoned.

Although it may not be the way they did it in the "old days," there is nothing wrong with marking down tidbits of useful information about players with whom you routinely interact. Greg Raymer, the 2004 WSOP main-event champion, is famous for this. Whether it's just a one-word descriptor (loose, tight, rock, or crazy) or a complete manuscript, whatever it takes for you to accurately describe an opponent's skills and abilities, playing style, and tendencies is fair game. I like to think of this information as human CliffsNotes.

I would suggest employing a little tact when writing down your findings, if only to keep your storage of data on the down low. For example, if you get hosed on a huge pot, don't immediately whip out a pen and paper and start scribbling away, all the while looking at the hand's victor and mumbling to yourself. Granted, there's nothing illegal about doing such a thing, but again, go for clandestine, not exhibition.

Internet poker players have it made in this respect. Forget about having to lay out note cards or a journal beside your computer screen; most online poker sites have a feature in their software package that actually allows for the taking of notes on individual players. Then, when you next encounter one or more of those players at your table, simply scan your personal database, find the name in question, and your notes will magically appear on screen, either in a column just off the online table or directly beside that player's avatar. Poker may be ancient, but when it comes to information, you can't beat technology.

# 31 BELIEVE IN YOURSELF

**C**onfidence is king. If you sit down at a poker table and don't expect to win, you absolutely should not be sitting down at that poker table in the first place. I can't tell you how many players I hear crying and whining mid-hand, fully expecting a forthcoming bad beat to oust them from a tourney or crush them in a cash game. When you belly up to the felt, you need to clear your mind of all negative thoughts and fully believe with every fiber of your being that you are going to have a huge day. Putting out a vibe that you are indeed a winner is the first step to actually becoming a winner.

You've no doubt heard the saying, "You are your own worst enemy." In the arena of confidence versus self-doubt, this is usually the biggest obstacle to anyone wanting to achieve success in any endeavor under the sun. If you don't believe in yourself, you can't possibly expect anyone else to believe in you. And given the solo nature of poker, with nobody else to rely upon, you will be either your greatest asset or your biggest drawback.

World-renowned self-help gurus like Anthony Robbins, Deepak Chopra, Dale Carnegie, Tom Butler-Bowdon, and Robin Sharma all have one thing in common: their emphasis is on getting their students and followers to embrace themselves. It's not just self-love, mind you, but self-worth. And though I'm far from knowledgeable on classic verse, there is a famous poem to that effect entitled "The Man Who Thinks He Can," attributed to Walter D. Wintle, which fits in perfectly with exuding confidence at the poker table. Two lines from the poem, which summarize the piece as a whole, read:

If you believe you can, you can.
If you think you are beaten, you are.

Of course, there is a world of difference between confidence and cockiness. Hyping yourself is fine, but believing your own hype beyond the practical is foolish and, ultimately, a recipe for disaster. No one is invincible.

# 32 CHARISMA CAN CHANGE THE COURSE OF HISTORY

If charisma can change the course of history—and the accomplishments of any world leader or outspoken civilian or celebrity will confirm this—surely it can change the outcome of a poker game. But charisma in this instance has nothing to do with playing style or the type of cards or hands you routinely play. This is all about attitude at the table, the willingness to really get involved in the game or, as some poker pundits might say, play "the game within the game."

Mixing it up with your opponents, either congenially or combatively, can open up many doors that would otherwise remain closed. You've heard the concept of "giving action to get action"; this is in the same realm but on a greater social level.

Charismatic players bring new energy to the game, and

their liveliness can often be contagious, quickly turning a humdrum table into the most happening stretch of felt in the entire card room. The action a charismatic player can create often comes in a mad rush, and if the game had been especially laggard prior, players might force the issue to get involved, even if their hands aren't quite up to snuff. Be aware of this tendency to join the fray and, if possible, capitalize on the haste of those players.

Also, if you are the charismatic player responsible for a game's new lifeblood, keep your eyes open to see whether other, more stolid players will perceive you as not only a nuisance or a distraction but also as an easy mark—your vim and vigor compensating for a lack of ability—and look to target you at their earliest opportunity. Use this to your advantage, and make them pay for doubting or misjudging your proficiency.

And then there are those players who simply cannot handle, for lack of a better term, a fun table. They require an unfriendly, cutthroat environment to play their best, and anything even remotely sociable takes them completely out of their game. Once again, be aware of these curmudgeonly players and monitor their temperament. If the new dimension the game takes appears to leave them out of sorts and vulnerable, look for an opening to strike.

Finally, while fresh energy can pump up a table and get things going, you also need to know when to throttle back and let things settle. Or, know when to let someone else carry the torch, and therefore, the crosshairs of ire. After a while, too much of anything gets annoying. Being the life of the party can be a good thing, but don't get married to that role. Remember, your goal is to separate your opponents from their chips, not to add your name to everyone's Christmas card list.

# 33 MONITOR YOUR PROGRESS (OR LACK THEREOF)

Golfers use a handicap system, bowlers have averages, and baseball, football, basketball, and hockey players have statistics for every facet of their games. This information isn't compiled just because it looks good on the back of trading cards; the numbers allow players (not to mention the organizations they play for, as well as their fans) to monitor their progress. For some, the stats will be inspiring. For others, they may be humbling or downright humiliating. But one thing the numbers won't do is lie. This is especially true in poker.

Stats can be misleading in some sports. In football, a perfectly thrown pass that bounces off the hands of the intended receiver and winds up in the hands of a defender still goes down as an interception, charged to the quarterback. But in poker, you're either winning, losing, or break-ing even. End of story.

Even if note-taking is not your thing, I would strongly suggest keeping track of your buy-ins and cash-outs, for both tournaments and cash-games. Granted, it's easy enough to monitor your successes and failures by how much money you remove from your pocket when you get home, but if you truly want to track your progress, exact figures will make a world of difference, especially over an extended period of time. And the minuscule time it takes for you to mark down dollar amounts prior to the start of your poker sessions and immediately following them is nothing compared with the information it will ultimately provide you.

Some players actually prefer not to keep an accurate re-cord of their winnings and losses simply because the num-bers are, shall we say, troubling. But if that's the case, it's abundantly clear you are doing far more harm than good by ignoring the information.

From a tax standpoint, especially if you have any desire to attempt to play poker for a living, keeping accurate re-cords of all your poker-related finances is imperative. The IRS has been known to come down hard on those who at-tempt to hide their earnings, and professional gamblers are at the very top of their watch list. By monitoring the com-ings and goings of your poker-related funds, not only will you avoid trouble with the bean-counters in black, you might actually save a few bucks in expenses.

Thus, the only reason you could possibly have for not keeping staunch poker records is laziness. And since poker and money essentially are joined at the hip, the very word "laziness" and any term or phrase associated with it should never be a part of a poker-related conversation.

# 34 LIE, CHEAT, AND STEAL—IT'S LEGAL

**O**kay, maybe not cheating, but lying and stealing are completely acceptable in poker. After all, the game is all about trickery and deception, and taking complete advantage of every situation is key. If you've got the stone-cold mortal lock, the next step is fleecing your opponent(s) out of the maximum number of chips. Conversely, if you've got absolutely nothing but are too heavily invested in the hand to fold, it's imperative that you make your opponent believe you've got the goods. And chances are you can't do either without pulling the wool over someone's eyes.

When it comes to consequentialism and "the ends justifying the means," Machiavelli had politics in mind, but his ideas fit poker perfectly. Short of using the old "Smith & Wesson beats four aces" technique—which is highly frowned upon by the management of any legal card room or casino—anything and everything you can do to move the chips from the center of the poker table to the space directly in front of you without drawing the ire of the "eye-in-the-sky" professionals is acceptable.

It's this "X-factor" characteristic that makes poker a game at which anyone can succeed. So what if you're not particularly good with numbers or memorizing ratios and statistics? If you're adept at reading people and situations and have the moxie to pull the trigger whenever you sense weakness, poker can reward you unlike any other game, sport, or hobby on the planet.

But successful deception requires more than just an analytical mind and the stones to act upon your scrutiny. You'll need to possess a touch of the dramatic; not Oscar-caliber, but just enough to bolster whatever measure of strength—or weakness—you attempt to convey.

For example, you should think about the different outcomes before the moment of truth arrives. There's no need to rush—take your time and play out the possibilities in your head. Then, when your course has been decided, begin planting the seeds early so that you can cultivate them properly when the time comes.

Even online poker—where players are essentially hidden from one another—relies heavily on smoke and mirrors. Because the players cannot interact directly as they would in brick-and-mortar card rooms, the trickery and deception is confined to betting ploys, be they outward shows of aggression or passive-aggressive trapping plays.

Regardless of the game's venue, the skill level of the players involved, and the mathematical science that is forever changing the manner in which the game is played, the legal sham and deceit ploys that experienced rounders can use to their advantage will keep the traditions of poker, spawned in the smoky backrooms of saloons and taverns, alive and well for eons to come.

# 35 HAVE A STRATEGY— BUT KNOW WHEN TO ABANDON IT

Having a game plan in place prior to the start of a contest or sporting event is a wise and prudent course of action. Boxers and mixed–martial artists usually enter a fight with a strategy that's been rehearsed for months. Baseball teams select their starting pitchers days before the first pitch is thrown. Football teams often open a game with a series of scripted plays. And even some of the most successful poker players favor beginning a session with a definite approach, especially for the final tables of major tournaments, where they know who their opponents are slated to be and what their strengths, weaknesses, and tendencies are. However, an inflexible attitude will undoubtedly result in destruction. If you're not astute enough to realize when a planned strategy isn't working, the only thing you can guarantee is a loss.

In poker parlance, changing your game plan is called shifting gears. For example, if the original plan was to come out raising with the specific intent of stealing blinds and forcing the other players to tighten up, but every one of your raises is met with a re-raise, unless you change your style quickly, you'll be on the rail or at the ATM in no time.

That doesn't mean you should veer away from your strategy completely. After all, if you've put any amount of thought into your plot, or in-depth study into your opponents, simply throwing away all that valuable reconnaissance work is foolish. But if you're not willing to accept that some changes to your master plan will have to be made immediately, the result will be the same as not having prepared at all.

The phrase "change brings unrest," though originally coined to describe emerging governments and fledgling national policies, can be applied directly to these scenarios. The reality is, most people hate change. It's disruptive and often confusing. Change forces people out of their element—their comfort zones—and requires them to chart a new course. And although this is almost always an unsettling process (to say the least) at the onset, the results can be far superior to those that would have come from the original plan.

However, switching gears is not for the faint of heart. Saying it and doing it are two very different things. And some poker players simply aren't capable of adopting a new strategy mid-game. Unfortunately, if those who cannot make transitions are looking for answers to the reasons behind their losing sessions, the truth is staring them right in the face—directly linked to their inflexibility.

Especially considering the millions of new players who have taken to the game of poker, all embodying myriad strategies and sensibilities, rolling with the punches is the only way to give yourself a legitimate chance of winning each time you take a seat at the table. Thinking you're going to power through the field, be it a cash game or a tournament, using exactly the same tactics every single time is the stuff of myth and legend. Maybe it would have worked years ago, just like Brazilian jiu-jitsu was the end-all martial art for UFC fighters when the competition was in its infancy. But now players need to bring a mixed bag of skills and abilities into the fray or, just like in the UFC, they're going to get knocked out or tapped out before they know what hit 'em.

# 36 BE A NINJA—NEVER LET THEM SEE YOU COMING

It wasn't their skills with the sword or shuriken that made ninjas so effective; it was their ability to sneak up on their enemies, even when their enemies knew they were coming. Poker players should follow their lead, remaining hidden— even in plain sight—until the last possible moment.

If a martial arts reference is too obscure for you, consider the great boxers of our time. The best of the best, like Muhammad Ali, never telegraphed their punches. Instead, they would dance around, jockeying for position, and then, when the opportunity presented itself, *wham!* They'd strike with power and precision, and it was lights out for their opponents.

Many poker players make their intentions known long before they act, often giving their adversaries more than

enough time to plot a counterattack. Whether it's a relatively small tell, like fiddling with their chips or cards (preparing to raise or fold), or something far more obvious like
becoming visibly excited or disgruntled, at a table with even
reasonably keen and aware players, this will be a dead giveaway. And once your opponents catch on to your pre-action
antics, they'll be watching you like a hawk, waiting for you
to tip your hand.

If you can control your actions and emotions, you may
be able to use this ability to your advantage by purposely
emoting some semblance of elation or disgust, thereby dis-
pensing false information to your opponents and hammer-
ing them when they take the bait. Chances are this will only
work once, so if you do decide to try it, make it count; you
won't get a second opportunity.

But rather than try to turn a bad situation into a good
one, you're much better off simply controlling yourself from
the start. Some poker players refuse to look at their cards
until it's their turn to act so that they can completely avoid
divulging any information, no matter how severe their opponents' scrutiny. Howard "the Professor" Lederer is among
this group of "late-lookers." Even though he's one of the best
at masking emotions, his decision to wait until the last moment to study his cards leaves nothing to chance.

Because poker is a game of peaks and valleys, often with
severe swings between the heights and depths, players need
to take advantage of every opportunity they possibly can.
Thus, when you're dealt a big hand and you finally have the

chance to win a big pot, don't compromise your position by giving away your strength too soon. On the other hand, if your hand is weak, or if your draw comes up short, don't make it too obvious or your opponents will bet you out of the hand—a hand that, though substandard, may still have been strong enough to win you the pot.

Finally, although poker usually boils down to strength and weakness—one hand trumping another—adding covert elements to your game will result in your dragging additional pots or larger pots, pots you wouldn't have normally won, and pots that would not normally have been nearly so large.

# 37 STAY COOL UNDER PRESSURE

**P**oker and Wild West duels from back in the day have much in common. Ironically, more than a few of those duels were the result of happenings at poker games. But of all their similarities, one snippet of advice for the combatants of either reigns supreme: stay cool under pressure.

Rudyard Kipling, one of the most famous writers of the twentieth century, began an oft-recited passage, "If you can keep your head when all about you / Are losing theirs . . ." Considering the context to which I'm applying it, the stanza doesn't require completion. The bottom line is that whether you've flopped the nuts and are simply trying to get paid off, or you've missed your draw by a country mile and have most of your chips committed, staying calm will definitely yield far greater results than falling to pieces.

When it comes to poker, you can't get emotional. Financial experts say the same thing about money. The correlation is perfect, because poker is also about money (winning it and losing it). So if you're the type that doesn't handle pressure well, perhaps you should look into a different pastime or career; poker will not be kind to those with high blood pressure.

No matter the situation, panic will never give you a happy ending. Whether you get slightly flustered or totally lose your mind is irrelevant—if just a hint of dread-inspired confusion creeps in, the enemy has already breached the perimeter.

Keep in mind, when you sit at a poker table, there are always eyes upon you, waiting for you to crumble and break under the strain. Some players have been waiting for this moment: one may have been exhibiting an otherwise passive existence until someone else shows their vulnerability, and then it's like a lion on a wounded gazelle.

Situations such as these are relatively easy to spot. A player gets flustered, often due to a bad beat, and then compounds the problem by immediately trying to push the action in an effort to regain his prior standing. Maybe he lost too much (perhaps more than he could afford), or maybe he simply allowed ego to override intelligence. Whatever the case, by allowing the moment to overwhelm you, short of a miracle, recovery is virtually impossible.

The trick isn't realizing when you're in a funk, for by then the damage is already done. No, it's identifying the situation before it comes to pass, nipping it in the bud, and preventing any real (or additional) damage from occurring. Think of yourself as a fighter jet hit by enemy fire. If you can regain level flight before dipping below the horizon, there is still hope. But once you drop past the point of no return, a crash is imminent, and no parachute will save you.

# 38 EXPAND YOUR HORIZONS

**P**oker has never been more popular than it is right now. Chris Moneymaker's 2003 World Series of Poker main-event victory opened up the floodgates, and the game has grown by leaps and bounds around the globe since. But more than just a new wave of players, there is now an overwhelming array of tutorial devices on the market—books, videos, and DVDs, online programs and training software, and even live multiday "boot camps" that can be taken advantage of to vastly improve poker skills.

To select the material that's best for you, first make an honest assessment of your current skill level. Attending lectures on advanced tournament strategies if you're only a $0.25/$0.50 home game player will be a colossal waste of time. The same goes for reading a book or watching a

DVD on low-limit cash game tactics if you're trying to bolster your tournament play. Think of your focus in the poker world—not what you'd like to do but what you're currently doing—and try to strengthen that area of your game first.

Most of the big-name professional poker players have at least one book or DVD in circulation. Choose the player whose style you admire, and more important, one that resembles your own (even remotely), or one that, tactically, you can relate to. Otherwise, you may find yourself trying to pull off maneuvers that, though you fully understand them, simply don't commingle well with your style. With so many professional players achieving household-name status these days, there's no reason to stop at picking just one pro. Chances are each of the players you admire has something the others don't; amassing as much knowledge as possible from the experts who play poker for a living against the toughest competition day in and day out will take your game to the next level no matter where your current ability lies.

Most of the online poker sites offer training tables, free play tables, and a wide variety of teaching implements—everything from odds calculators to statistical databases on every imaginable facet of the game. Along these same lines, most of the brick-and-mortar card rooms also offer teaching tables; if you're new to organized poker (if you've only been playing in home games prior), even if you think you know everything there is to know about the game, put your ego on the shelf, take a seat, and see if you can pick up a nugget or two.

Specialized training software, geared primarily for tournament players, allows for the customization of many aspects—everything from the number of players to varying skill levels to starting chip stacks. By running simulations, exposing yourself to as many situations as possible, you'll have a decided advantage when those scenarios arise during live play.

Finally, from a value standpoint, the live tutorials in the form of one-day and multiday "boot camps" are the best. These offer hands-on instruction from some of the best players in the game. Another benefit is the "graduation tournaments," limited to players in the boot camp, which give you a chance not only to put your new knowledge to the test but also to possibly win some great prizes (from $$$ to major poker event entries). Perhaps the best aspect of these semi-private sessions is the networking opportunities they provide, connecting you with like-minded individuals who are serious about improving their skills. More than a few poker "focus groups" have been formed as a result of these gatherings.

Despite all the improvement ammunition out there, if you have the attitude that you've already achieved your poker peak and there's nothing you can do to improve, I guarantee you there's not a product out there that will help you except for a slice of humble pie.

# 39 ADMIRE THE PROS, DON'T MIMIC THEM

Turn on the television and flick through the channels, and you're bound to stumble across a poker program sooner or later. *High Stakes Poker, Poker After Dark, World Series of Poker*—there are now so many high-profile programs and events, it wouldn't surprise me if poker had a dedicated network before long. And with the extensive coverage comes the opportunity to continually observe many of the world's most accomplished players in their element, doing what they do best. But there's one major caveat to that exposure: oftentimes, the everymen of the poker world—that's you, me, and everyone else who isn't playing for millions of dollars on a regular basis—take their admiration just a wee bit too far.

Don't misunderstand, there's absolutely nothing wrong

with wanting to emulate Phil Ivey, Daniel Negreanu, Doyle Brunson, or any of the other professional poker greats out there. However, it's important you realize that those players are one of a kind. They've earned their stripes, paying their dues over years of cash game and tournament play. They've battled innumerable opponents on every continent, facing virtually every poker-related situation imaginable over and over again. As such, the ploys they use are expertly calculated and perfectly executed. So when Tom "Durrrr" Dwan shoves one million dollars over the top of Barry Greenstein's raise holding a measly 9-2 off-suit, he knows exactly what he's doing. What's more, his reputation garners him respect, and Greenstein lays down his superior hand (in that case, pocket tens).

Now, if you try that same move at your next home game, shoving $100 with Ace-Jack, don't be surprised if you get called in three spots. You're not Tom Dwan or any other superstar player whose game you have come to admire and respect. To be them, you'd have to possess the same sensibilities, have shared identical experiences, and read situations equally as well. There are no shortcuts to acquiring these skills. You should strive to be the best player you can possibly be, creating your own style, honing your skills while playing your brand of poker, and perhaps one day you'll find yourself seated across from your poker idol, battling heads-up for the World Series of Poker's main-event championship bracelet.

# 40 AVOID BEING THE SMALL FISH IN A BIG POND

In poker, chips equal power. The more chips you have, the more powerful you are. For the most part, this relates directly to cash games, since competitors in tournaments start with an equal-sized stack.

Some tournaments (usually small buy-in affairs) reward patronage with bonus chips. Play live poker at that establishment for a few hours before the tourney begins, and you'll receive "x" amount of additional chips. Unless you plan on amassing all the hours and bonus chips possible, tournaments such as these should be avoided at all costs. You don't ever want to short-stack yourself, especially if you're paying the same entry fee as those players who will be starting off with more chips. Some might argue that a few chips won't make a difference, but if you consider the effect of a double-up, and a double-up after that, a few hundred chips can equal a few thousand in no time, especially in No Limit.

Similarly, I'd suggest avoiding re-buy tournaments as well. Although players generally start with equal stacks, those competitors with deeper pockets have a decided advantage. In fact, if more cash-heavy competitors wanted to play like absolute donkeys for a few rounds to accumulate chips quickly and let luck take its course, they actually have a significant advantage over those players trying to play solid poker. Remember, you can win pot after pot, but if you lose one big one (especially in No Limit Hold'em, played in most tournaments these days), your entire stack could be gone in a flash. And if you were planning on tackling the tournament on just one entry, game over.

From a value perspective, where confining your play to a single buy-in puts you in an event with a very large prize pool (which most re-buy tournaments boast) on the cheap, you would definitely be getting your money's worth. But you also first need to decide whether navigating the minefield that re-buy tournaments usually turn out to be is worth your initial investment. Some might prefer a standard format, where a previously eliminated player cannot come back from the dead to eliminate them. Again, it just depends on your perception of risk versus value, what you are willing to give up and what you're looking to get.

In the realm of cash games, the size of your starting stack is extremely important. Think of your chips as ammunition and the poker game as a gunfight. You certainly don't want to go into combat low on ammo. If anything, you want as much as your opponents, but it's far better to have more.

In Limit Hold'em, this doesn't really factor in, as your bet amounts are limited to the preset stakes. However, sitting down with a large stack of chips can convey confidence and bravado: you're an aggressive player, willing to mix it up and take chances. This could earn you some respect before you play a single hand. Conversely, sitting down with a small stack can convey a lack of confidence; you're relatively unsure about your game and are afraid to risk more. This could result in your being targeted by more experienced players.

In No Limit Hold'em, there are two decidedly different schools of thought. Some players enjoy playing "small stack poker," sitting down at a table with the minimum buy-in—usually far less than any of the other players have—and waiting to get it all in on a single good hand. Sometimes referred to as push poker, players employing this strategy are often looking to "hit 'n' run"—that is, they're looking to double up and leave.

The major problem with starting off with a stack too small is that unless your hand is strong and defendable, you have no margin of error. It's all or nothing all the time. And even if you do decide to make a stand and push, if your stack size doesn't frighten your opponents, you may receive more callers than you had hoped, thus considerably reducing your odds of winning.

Therefore, the best way to attack a No Limit Hold'em

game is to join with at least as many chips as the largest stack at the table. Like fighting fire with fire, you want your weapons to be as menacing as those you are facing. That might require dropping to lower stakes, but the grandeur associated with the table or game shouldn't be the reason you play. You should select a table that you can victimize, or at least where you have a better shot at winning. Bottom line: you want to be the big fish in a small pond, not the other way around.

# 41 RAISE IN THE BEGINNING FOR FREE CARDS AT THE END

**P**oker, like chess, involves deep thought and strategic planning. If you can think at least one move ahead of your opponents, barring anything completely out of the ordinary, the scales of fortune should tip in your favor. And because poker is also heavily steeped in the concept of money management, any maneuvering you can undertake to play cost effectively is well worth the effort. By linking these two understandings, you can become an extremely formidable player, regardless of the game (Limit or No Limit) or the stakes.

For example, let's say you're in late position with suited connectors or any similar drawing-type hand. By raising before the flop, you should be able to get the turn card for free, and possibly even the river depending on your opponents' holdings, their style of play, and the forthcoming board. If the flop brings you a big draw—straight draw, flush draw, straight and flush draws, or the whole enchilada, an open-ended straight flush draw—you have a few options: if the flop is checked to you, you can simply check and get the turn for free. If the flop is checked to you, you can make a semi-bluff—you're still drawing, but depending on your number of outs, you may be favored—and possibly even take the pot down right there. Or, if an early position play-er bets the flop, you can raise. As this may have just been a "test-the-waters" maneuver by the early position player, your raise (again, a semi-bluff) may end it right there. At the very least, it should get you the river for free—assuming the turn is of no help to either of you.

It is unlikely that a raise pre-flop followed by a check on both the flop and the turn will bear much fruit—unless your opponent misreads the situation and you catch your card on the river. In that case, he may actually bet out—ei-ther he thinks he needs to bet to win, or he made his hand as well—and you now have the opportunity to raise. What's more, if your opponent has nothing and feels he needs to get you to fold to win, he may just re-raise you, hoping you were pushing air. By now, you've seen the flop, turn, and river all for the price of a single raise before the flop, and if you've connected, you're actually going to get rewarded for your prescience. But even if you end up losing the hand, whether to a made hand or from folding because your draw didn't materialize, it's a prime example of how being aggressive on early streets can reward you later in the hand.

For the record, this same play can be done from early position. Because many players try to trap after hitting their hand, an early position pre-flop raise with the same type of drawing hand (suited connectors or similar) should not only disguise your hand's strength (many players, especially the tighter ones, only choose to raise in early position with medium- or large-pocket pairs or big aces) but also cause your opponents to respect—or even fear—a check on the flop, expecting you to check-raise them if they dare bet.

The most important aspect is identifying the types of players you're battling against. Fearless, aggressive players will likely try to control the action and probably won't be so quick to consistently allow free cards from pre-flop check-raises. But if you find yourself competing against less-experienced, less-confident, or otherwise timid players, you might be able to use this technique throughout the session with phenomenal results.

# 42 SHOW ONE, SHOW ALL

There's nothing wrong with showing your cards to your opponents every now and then, especially if you're trying to establish a certain table image (tight, loose, maniac, et cetera). Although I'm not a big fan of the practice—poker is all about information, and the less your opponents know about you and the types of hands you play, the better—if there's a method to your madness, then by all means, go for it.

Some players will show their hands after their opponent has folded, a "courtesy-show," as if to say: "Good fold, I had you." When this happens, even if you weren't involved in the hand, make sure you get to see those cards. If the player doesn't show you directly, ask the dealer to expose them. You're entitled. By the same token, if you show an opponent your cards, don't make a fuss if other players want to see them; even if they weren't in the hand, they're entitled. Once you've decided to show your hand, better to just toss your cards face up on the felt for all to see and be done with it.

For some players, showing cards has nothing to do with courtesy and everything to do with provoking a reaction. In this respect, they'll show their hand after a successful bluff, rubbing the loser's nose in it. Again, I'm not a big fan of revealing information, but there is a time and a place for everything. If you think a player is fragile enough that he could be put on tilt by your exposing a bluff that cost him a big pot, doing so may be well worth it. But don't be surprised if any of your future plays or weaker hands get picked off—you may inadvertently have labeled yourself as a bluffer, even if it was the first and only time you tried it.

Another thing to be on the lookout for is "neighbor shows." This is just like it sounds—when a player at the table gives his neighbor a peek at his hole cards before tossing them into the muck. Once again, you have a right to see those cards. Even if neither player was involved in the hand—for example, neither committed a bet to the pot on that specific hand—you could argue that one player seeing the cards another player doesn't play is the same as seeing the cards he does play. A dealer may tell you you're wrong, but a floorman—who is usually more knowledgeable of the rules—will most likely decide in your favor.

Demanding a "show one, show all" may draw a player's

ire, or that of the rest of the table, but you're not there to make friends—you're there to win money. Besides, speaking up may cause the table to be a little less show 'n' tell, which, if you are one of the stronger players in the game, will work to your advantage. You may be able to read situations or players without having to see their hole cards, whereas other players may not.

While the "show one, show all" rule is designed to promote table equality and not be a cause for conflict, it quite often causes a stir. Be aware of players who have issues with this rule. Chances are, they need all the extra help they can get, and you may be able to target them later.

# 43 PLAYING WELL MEANS LAYING DOWN WINNERS

To put it mildly, you can't call every bet. While you'd undoubtedly like to—with no consequences to your chip stack, of course—that simply isn't a viable option. Thus, there will be times when you absolutely have to fold your hand, even though you're probably laying down the winner. But don't think of this as a sign of weakness—think of it as a confirmation that you are playing smart poker.

From a simple percentage standpoint, you cannot win every hand you play. Sure, it's mathematically possible, but far from likely. And if that's true, then it's also true that you cannot be ahead in every hand you play. Therefore, some of the hands you play cannot be taken to term—you'll need to lay them down at some point.

If you're predominantly a tight player, laying down

hands is nothing new—you fold far more than you play. From hand selection pre-flop, to his actions on the flop and turn, to his final act on the river, a tight player will be less likely to chase draws or pursue anything less than the stone-cold nuts, so dumping a hand that isn't a guaranteed winner is a piece of cake. But for looser players, players ready and willing to gamble, pursuing draws that don't get there but catching a card that results in some semblance of a hand—a hand that may still be the best one out there—laying it down may be a serious bone to be chewed.

Still, at what point do you draw the line? For example, say you kept track of every draw you chased where you didn't catch the card or cards you were looking for (to make a straight or a flush) but instead wound up with a pair or two pairs. If you decided to call every river bet, no matter how large, to take the guesswork out of the game, what do you think your poker-related finances would look like? I'll tell you—you wouldn't be playing poker anymore, that's for sure.

I've said it before and I'll say it again, if only to convey the importance of the concept: poker is not all about making hands, outwitting your opponents, or having guts—it's all about money management, making the correct percentage plays time after time. If you allow smart fiscal sense to override your ego, over time, you will be a winning player.

# 44 FINANCIALLY SPEAKING, CHARITY TOURNAMENTS ARE TERRIBLE

**D**on't get me wrong, charity tournaments are a lot of fun and, should you be fortunate enough to win one, can be extremely profitable. However, in my opinion, the cons far outweigh the pros to the point that you'd be much better off investing the money in a different type of tournament.

From a "rubbing-elbows-with-celebrities" standpoint, charity tournaments cannot be beat. Because of the world-wide poker explosion, superstars from the entertainment, sports, political, and of course, the poker realms flock to these events en masse, all more than happy to donate to a great cause and have a little fun in the process, not to mention get their pictures snapped for posterity. So if you want a free pass to an otherwise unobtainable red carpet, charity tournaments are the ticket. But when it comes to poker value, I'd strongly suggest looking elsewhere.

For one thing, most charity tournaments have a less-than-favorable format. You don't get a lot of chips to start with and the rounds are not all that long, either. Also, every charity tournament I know of is a re-buy event—with the emphasis on re-buy. Remember, these events are about raising money, not rewarding poker excellence, so the more money in the prize pool, the better. Competitors are usually encouraged to play fast and loose, and table talk—containing gobs of posturing and goading—is intended to spark action. Of all the charity events I have been involved with or taken part in, I have yet to discover a deep-pocketed participant who didn't play like a maniac, happily spreading chips around like a tornado displacing mobile homes. For some charity competitors, it comes down to an ego fest—whoever can spend the most money and look like the biggest hero. Again, there's nothing wrong with that mentality—it's all for a good cause—but if you're looking for a tournament where a single buy-in gives you a decent shot at winning, charity events are not for you.

Back on the subject of prize pools, in regular tournaments, all the money in the prize pool (save any that may be removed for the dealers) is returned to the players. In charity tournaments, only half the prize pool (and in some cases, less) is actually paid out. Granted, you may be able to write off your entry fee from your taxes (or half the fee; consult your accountant), but again, if you're looking for value, paying more and winning less just doesn't cut it.

As a whole, poker tournaments are usually relatively quiet affairs, allowing the competitors some measure of peace to concentrate on their game. After all, there's big money at stake. That's not the case with charity tournaments. There's usually an emcee—a celebrity, often from the poker world—walking around, commentating on the action, keeping the people excited and the action (and the chips) moving. I've even been to events where bands and DJs were playing in the same room. Obviously, this is far from the norm of a regular poker tournament, but then again, charity poker tournaments are far from the norm.

Finally, for the winners of the events—and all those who place in the money—there is often considerable pressure on them to donate at least some of their winnings back to the hosting charity. This scenario seldom unfolds in a direct manner—although I have personally witnessed a host walking up to the event's winner with his hand out, all the while saying into the microphone: "So, (X), how much are you going to donate?"—but there is usually an overwhelming blitz of peer pressure, to which the victors almost always cave.

Bottom line: if you're looking for a poker charity tournament, find the best event for the money, one that offers a solid structure and an adequate starting stack, where you can concentrate and play your best.

# 45 WALK IT OFF

Let's say you've just experienced a horrific bad beat by an idiotic player who clearly got once-in-a-blue-moon lucky against you. Rather than sit there and stew and, in all probability, let your aggravation dictate your play for at least the next few hands—but more likely the rest of the session—get up from the table and take a walk. Granted, leaving the table isn't going to take the sting out of what's just happened, but staying put will likely compound the problem when you try to get even with the offending donkey by targeting him in the coming hands, most likely with cards that you wouldn't normally play (or have any business playing) in the first place.

Throwing good money after bad, while understandable considering Man's inclination toward revenge (especially at the poker table), is one of the worst things any poker player can do. A close second to playing while impaired and under the influence, playing while tilted is a disaster in the making. It doesn't matter if you know your nemesis is ripe for a fall based on the foolish play he just pulled off against you; this is a given. Nor does it matter that he has a ton of chips in front of him at the moment and you want to strike before he distributes them around the table; pursue a hand you shouldn't out of payback, and he will certainly have more. The only thing that matters is that you recognize—and quickly—the mindset you're in and get away from the action before that mindset transforms a bad situation into a horrendous one.

But beyond your "cooling-off period," there's another solid reason to step away for a bit—you're giving your enemy a chance to replay the scene in his head. If anything, you want that donkey to get back to his "business-as-usual" style of play. Let him keep playing like an idiot—perhaps the only way he knows how—and when you get back in the game and the two of you tangle again, play the percentages, and the result will (hopefully) be different. By allowing him to see your angst, it might just dawn on him that he did pull a rabbit out of the hat, and now that you (and everyone else at the table) are gunning for him, he's going to tighten up his play or, even worse, cash out.

Let him enjoy his moment in the sun. Chances are, moments like that for him are few and far between. Don't give him an incentive to leave; it's for this reason I never berate a player who stomped me, no matter how humiliating the beat down. I want him feeling all safe and secure with no fear of reprisal. I want him thinking his play was smart and righteous and I was the moron who was chasing. Then, when he least expects it—which will be always—he'll get stuck in a situation he cannot extricate himself from, and I'll get all my chips back, and more.

So get up, chill out, take a walk, have a drink, use the restroom; give yourself at least a one hundred count or so—whatever it takes to flush your system of all that negative energy. And then, when your heartbeat has returned to an even rhythm, get back in the game and take the fool down.

# 46 BE THE TRAPPER, NOT THE TRAPPEE

**F**lopping monster hands is a dream scenario every poker player prays for ad nauseam. However, flopping a huge hand is one thing; if you fail to get paid off on that monster, it's all for naught. For this reason, some players opt not to push the action from the onset and wait instead—hoping is more like it—for their opponents to make a hand or, at the very least, initiate the betting. Then they can spring a trap and rake in the dough. The only problem with that little ploy? Oftentimes the trapper becomes the trappee.

For example, let's say you're holding two small hearts—suited connectors, perhaps—and the flop brings all hearts. As you already know, flopping a flush is a rarity—118:1—and you certainly don't want to see it go to waste, so you decide to slow-play the action, hoping other players in the hand, especially those holding one big heart, will pursue their draws. But while your thinking is understandable, it's also fraught with peril. A small flush, while impressive, is still just a small flush. If one more heart hits the board, chances are you're not only beat, but should someone make a big bet, you're now faced with an extremely uncomfortable decision. And then there's the possibility that players holding two pairs or a set will make a full house and, once again, push out a big bet that you may be inclined to call. By slow-playing your made hand, you have allowed a lesser hand to get there—for free—and now instead of stacking chips, you're forced to re-buy. In essence, your trap trapped you!

This all boils down to the age-old "a bird in the hand versus two in the bush" philosophy. If you're in early position with a flopped flush, you're much better off betting out, thus forcing any players who want to draw to pay for their prospects. Or, in the event that someone has a bigger flush—another legitimate possibility—you can at least make that discovery early on, before you have too much invested, and get away from the hand with minimal damage. Another potential scenario is that a player behind you, thinking your wager is just a feeler bet or at most a semi-bluff (perhaps he put you on a pair with a draw), will raise in the hopes of getting you to check the turn, in which case he can then check right behind you (if he was drawing) and get to see the river for free.

Then there's the scenario that checking a flopped monster will result in a free turn card that completely kills your action—for example, a fourth card of the same suit or, in the event you flopped a straight, another connecting card that fills in the sequence. Now, even if a player has two pairs or a set, getting him to call any bet you make will be a tough sell. Furthermore, if he doesn't have much invested in the pot—your previous check assisted in that endeavor—getting away from his hand shouldn't be too difficult.

Bottom line: make money whenever you can. If you're ahead, get your chips in the pot. Make your opponents get lucky to beat you. And if they do, shrug it off as one of the pitfalls of poker. However, force them to pay for that privilege. It will enable you to collect some valuable information about the other players around you: who's tight, who's loose, and, should you decide to try trapping later in the session, who will pay you off.

# 47 BLUFFING SHOULD COMPLEMENT YOUR STYLE OF PLAY, NOT DEFINE IT

There's no arguing that bluffing an opponent (or, even better, multiple opponents) out of a huge pot is extremely satisfying. It all hearkens back to the theft and deception mentality that the game of poker so strongly embodies. But invigorating as it is to get a player to lay down a better hand, you're much better off being known as a great all-around poker player rather than just a great bluffer.

Case in point: a well-known professional poker player and WSOP main-event champion fancies himself the best bluffer in the No Limit Hold'em arena. To his credit, he's extremely good—beyond good, actually—a fact he's proven time and time again on national television against many of the best poker players on the planet. But there's an enormous downside to his devious antics: players go out of their way to make calls against him—very loose calls, in fact—hoping to beat him at his own game. He's become a major target, a "big-game trophy," that less-accomplished players want to beat at all costs and brag about to anyone who will listen. So now, in hands that he probably should have won, with his trickster reputation preceding him wherever he plays, even players with the weakest of holdings make calls against him and ultimately beat him. Although this has worked to his advantage many times on the cash game front where a player can be patient and wait for opportunities, out on the tournament circuit, where a player is forced to play far more hands (though still many less than ideal), an early trip to the rail has been the usual result. In fact, he hasn't even come remotely close to duplicating his 2006 feat, whereby he cut through a field of 8,773 players en route to a record $12 million payday. Once again, his bluffing skills are first-rate—and yours might be, too—but getting labeled as an exceptional faker, as history has shown, will eventually lose its luster, thereby making wins that much harder to come by—wins that would have been in the bag otherwise.

To that effect, having other players respect the entirety of your game—bluffing, reading skills, ability to switch gears, creativity, patience, ability to make big lay-downs, et cetera—will provide you with a much better platform from which you can make all sorts of moves without being targeted for doing one specific thing perpetually.

Robert Anson Heinlen, the "dean of science-fiction writers," said that "specialization is for insects." Applying his sentiment to the poker world makes perfect sense. When you consider where insects are on the food pyramid—at or near the bottom—possessing a jack-of-all-trades capability is a much better way to go.

# 48 ACT LIKE YOU'VE BEEN THERE BEFORE

In poker, the swings of fortune and misfortune are unlike anything else, save for a commodities broker riding the roller coaster between market surges and margin calls. As such, it's an emotional game. And there's nothing wrong with showing your emotions at the table, be they elation or desolation. But c'mon people, check yourself before you wreck yourself.

Although televised poker has helped the game circle the globe like a wildfire through a dry forest, it has also contributed to one less-than-impressive aspect of the game by throwing a blinding spotlight on the after-hand celebration or tantrum.

Anyone who has watched the televised coverage of a final table from a major tournament has witnessed both sides of that scenario. For the victor, the thrill of victory: usually marked by arms raised with a crescendo of war whoop-screams, followed by a plethora of high-fives and shoulder-claps from supporting family and friends in the studio audience. And then there's the loser, and the agony of defeat: facial expressions akin to sucking on the last of a bushel of sour lemons, oftentimes accompanied by a brutal tirade or lecture toward the victor (poker superstar Phil Hellmuth after a bad beat comes to mind). Although some may argue these antics come with the territory, others would be quick to point out that, passion and agitation aside, one can—and should—win with class or lose with dignity.

For many, especially the new crop of poker superstars like the regular Joes and Janes not used to being in the spotlight, becoming a polarizing figure, and in some cases a household name, was never anticipated when they embarked on their amateur to professional poker career. But because of the insane amount of money that has been infused into the game in recent years, poker has transcended simple hobby status, transforming some of the more popular players into legitimate cultural icons. Suddenly, these players are being watched, and not just by the poker community but by a younger generation looking for role models in every nook and cranny. As such, their actions will leave a lasting impression. And if that lasting impression is an ugly stain instead of a positive mark, the damage is tough, if not impossible, to undo.

Yes, poker players are doing everything within their power to take every last cent and chip from their opponents and send them skulking away with their tails between their legs. However, poker is also the only game in the world in which competitors can be genuinely congenial and conversational (if they so choose) in the midst of the most heated competition imaginable—rivalries that could result in huge fiscal windfalls or complete ruin in the blink of an eye. No other sport, game, or hobby on earth can make such a claim. It's for this reason that participating players, especially the giants of the game, should make every effort to bring some measure of civility to the table, if only to set a proper example and convey the type of sportsmanship the game truly deserves.

# 49 TOKE THE DEALER

This may seem like the most obvious tip of the bunch, but you'd be surprised how many players, including some who have been playing for years, aren't hip to the practice of tipping dealers.

The fact is, dealers work for tips. Forget the benefits associated with the casinos or card rooms in which they ply their trade. From a fixed hourly wage standpoint, a dealer's earnings are usually at or near the minimum legal limit; it's through tips that they earn their real bread and butter.

For many novice players making their first foray into organized, legal card rooms, tipping dealers is an alien concept. Chances are they didn't toke their home game card-slinger; they probably just skimmed a few dollars from pots here and there to cover the host's expenses. Unfortunately, even for some experienced players, tipping the dealer is a custom they don't believe in. In my opinion, that's akin to stiffing a waiter or waitress. They're working for your enjoyment, so the least you can do is thank them financially for their efforts.

Some players have trouble figuring out how much to tip. Contrary to popular belief, the size or stakes of the game do not dictate how much a dealer gets per hand. For example, watch any episode of *High Stakes Poker,* a televised game with nosebleed stakes and innumerable multi-hundred-thousand-dollar pots. Each player keeps a stack of redbirds ($5 chips) specifically for toking the dealer after a win. Sure, after raking a particularly monstrous pot, maybe they'll toss a little more, but for the most part, $5 is the standard tip.

Now, I've seen untelevised home games with a mountain of cash on the table where the dealer made some serious coin courtesy of tips. The largest single tip I ever witnessed was $7,000 on a hand that featured a royal flush beating a straight flush. Sick!

Conversely, the best tips, percentage-wise, are often awarded in the lower-limit games—$2/$4 and $3/$6 Hold'em; I've actually seen minuscule $15 and $20 pots result in $3 and $4 tips for the dealer. Granted, I've played in small-limit games where the hand-winner tossed the dealer a $1 chip and asked for a chop—breaking down the chip into smaller increments; in the case of a $1 chip, usually $0.50 is kept by the dealer and the other $0.50 is returned to the player—but many card rooms and casinos have grown tired of dealing with silver—loose change in dealers' racks or on the poker tables—and decreed $1 chips the minimum. While this has actually caused some players to curtail their tipping in those facilities, or at least reduced the frequency of their tips, for the most part, it has helped dealers improve their daily wages.

While I've heard of a few casinos and card rooms where dealers pool their tips, it's usually every man for himself. Overall, this is a much better practice: some dealers are faster and more efficient (dealing more hands per shift than their contemporaries, thereby receiving more tips), and some are simply nicer and friendlier, also garnering more "love." The best dealers are both fast and friendly; they run a smooth game with nary a hiccup and are well liked by all the seated players.

Bottom line: dealing poker is not the easiest profession in the world. Far from it. Hand-eye coordination helps. A solid understanding of math (especially when pots need to be split—a must for Omaha or High-Low Stud—or when side-pots need to be figured out) is also a necessity. Additionally, poker dealers need to have thick skin and a decent tolerance level; oftentimes, losing players (especially those experiencing a bad beat) will blame the dealer for their misfortune. But with the necessary skills and mental acuity, dealing poker can be a true career with a lengthy duration. Best of all, no two moments will ever be the same.

# 50 CHOP ONCE, CHOP ALWAYS

**C**hopping, a scenario that takes place only in cash games and never in tournaments, is when action has been folded around to the blinds, and rather than see a flop, both blinds agree to take their money back (minus any drop for the jackpot—if applicable—that may have been taken from the small blind) and go on to the next hand. More than anything, it's a courtesy play, a way of getting on with the action rather than having two players in so-called forced-action hands battling it out. That said, chopping should be an always-or-never maneuver. You don't chop for a few rounds and then, after looking down and finding a great hand, decide not to. Try that once and the entire table will gang up on you.

Then there's the karma angle to consider. I was playing in a $10/$20 No Limit cash game at the Bellagio. Great table, extremely congenial, with plenty of action. And as is often the case with $10/$20 NL, there was some serious money on the felt. Everyone at the table had been chopping their blinds since I sat down, roughly four hours prior to the scenario I'm about to relate. That's when a new player joined the game, taking the open seat next to an older man who had been playing ridiculously tight. The newcomer sat down just in time for his big blind, which he posted. All the players folded their cards in turn, leaving it up to the blinds: Mr. Tight and the 50-some-odd-year-old new addition in the big blind.

Mr. Newcomer took a quick look at his hand and asked Mr. Tight in the small blind if he wanted to chop.

"I never chop," said Mr. Tight.

I couldn't believe my ears, which I'm certain went for everyone else at the table. Mr. Tight had chopped for four hours straight, but now he wasn't having any of it. Something was obviously up.

"Okay, no problem," Mr. Newcomer said. "Do what you're gonna do."

At which point, Mr. Tight promptly raised Mr. New-comer's big blind, putting out $60. To my surprise, Mr. New-comer called. The flop was three small cards, and Mr. Tight bet $100. Again, Mr. Newcomer called. The turn was a jack. Now, Mr. Tight made a big bet—$500. Again, Mr. Newcomer called, nearly beating his opponent's chips into the pot. The river was another small card.

Mr. Tight shoved his entire stack—nearly $3,000—forward. "All-in," he said.

"In for a penny, in for a pound," Mr. Newcomer replied. "I call."

Mr. Tight proudly tabled pocket kings. Mr. Newcomer smiled, turned over his pocket aces.

Like I said, karma. Even with the best possible starting hand in Texas Hold'em, the newcomer was willing to chop. But Mr. Tight, breaking one of the oldest rules (it's an ethical rule, not a legal one) in the poker book, reneged and paid the price, to the tune of his entire stack.

Should the situation arise—to chop or not to chop— that's totally up to you, but once you choose a route, stick to it for the duration of the session no matter what cards you're dealt.

# 51 NOBODY RIDES FOR FREE

If I've said it once I've said it a thousand times—poker is less about cards and more about information. Those who have the intel will probably end up leaving the table as winners. Those who are deficient in that arena will, in all likelihood, be the ones making the contributions. Therefore, since information is the key, willingly providing any for free is a foolish endeavor.

To paint a clearer picture, poker players should think of themselves as taxi drivers. No driver in his right mind would take a fare to his destination just for the heck of it—they do it for money. Poker is the same way; if you want to play, you have to pay.

From an action standpoint, we've already established that betting is one of the best ways to obtain information.

On the basis of your opponents' responses to your bet, you can try to determine what they might be holding.

Checking, on the other hand, though beneficial when you're drawing and don't want to invest unnecessary funds in an otherwise as-yet-unmade hand, won't provide you with much data. For instance, just because another player checks behind you doesn't necessarily mean he has a weak hand; he may have a monster and is waiting for you to catch up so he can trap you. So, not only do you not learn anything about his holding, you may let him get there for free.

From a showdown standpoint, free reveals are, in my opinion, tactically silly. After all, you're playing poker, not show 'n' tell. If you're the caller, not the bettor, always make your opponent show first. Don't be goaded into showing your cards first, no matter what the situation is. This aspect doesn't matter if you show down and win the pot, but if your opponent shows first and you see that he has you beat, you can muck your hand with nobody at the table the wiser. Sure, someone will ask to see your hand every now and then, but more often, it'll remain facedown in the muck. You've undoubtedly heard the phrase "less is more"; this is one of those instances to which that mindset definitely applies.

Another "no-free-rides" scenario worth discussing involves pre-flop raises with no subsequent callers. Every now and then the blind stealer will show his hand—usually a big ace or a large pocket pair—as if to reassure the table that he had the goods and wasn't trying to make a move. My question: Why bother? Poker isn't about winning approval; it's about winning chips. If you have a strong hand and are inclined to raise and no one has the cards, guts, or willingness to call, they don't deserve to see your cards. Better to keep them wondering and guessing—perhaps even second-guessing, which could very well put them on tilt (yes, even from having their blind stolen; I've seen it happen many times)—so that next time, when you want action, they might oblige you.

No matter your strategy or playing style, it's imperative you remember that in even the friendliest of games, your mission is to fleece your opponents out of every last penny they have while protecting your own stash. Giving your adversaries any assistance in doing to you what you are trying to do to them makes no sense whatsoever. So, if they're not willing to pay the fare, make 'em walk. Nobody rides for free.

# 52 A CHIP AND A CHAIR

**W**ithout question, the most oft-used phrase in poker is "a chip and a chair," the card-player's equivalent of "If I'm still in, don't count me out." Primarily reserved for tournament action, it can also be applied to cash game players who are down to their final dollars. But beyond simply a metaphor for "it's not over till it's over," throughout the annals of poker history, there have actually been quite a few players who have taken this statement literally.

Years ago, while playing in a Limit Hold'em Tournament at the Bell Gardens, California–based Bicycle Casino, I found myself among the remaining forty players (four tables) in the field. One of those players, a cantankerous older gent, was down to his last green ($25) chip. Considering they were only paying the top thirty, it looked like the lone chipster would be coming up a little short of the money—and that's when his miracle run began. For the next few levels, he won every single hand he played. Not only did he make it to the money, he made it to the final table. Granted, he was dead last in chips upon arriving, but he was still in the hunt. From his nearly dead-and-buried "chip and a chair" to a nice payday, all in the span of a few hours—talk about a reversal of fortune! But the story doesn't end there. Somehow, he managed to make it to the final two players—against me, no less. Mano-a-mano, we were now virtually even in chips. Although I usually prefer to play tournaments out to the very end, if for no other reason than I enjoy the dynamics of playing heads-up poker, considering all the man had accomplished, I thought I'd be chivalrous and proposed we chop, splitting the first- and second-prize money dead even.

"Not a chance," he said. "I'm gonna win this tournament and there's nothing you can do to stop me."

Long story short, he was absolutely correct. No matter what I had, he had something better. No matter what ploy I tried, he sniffed it out and countered it. And before the round was halfway through, all the tourney's chips were now in front of him. So, does his win—and others like it— prove anything definitively? Of course not, for every situation is different. But the "chip and a chair" sentiment is something every poker player the world over should keep in mind when next they play.

Too often, many players experiencing bad luck early on in tournaments are quick to pack it in, burning off the rest of their chips on low percentage plays, when they should instead think things through a little more clearly and pick a spot to try to mount a comeback. Case in point: poker pro "Action Dan" Harrington and the 2007 World Poker Tour's Doyle Brunson North American Poker Championship at the Bellagio in Las Vegas. Harrington should have been gone in the first round of play; down to his last few chips he battled all the way back to take second place, winning more than $620,000 in the process.

So you see, anything is possible. And that's exactly what makes poker such an amazing game—a game that can be enjoyed by anyone, anywhere, at any stakes. No matter what the future holds, no matter what improvements technology brings to the world, poker and the very essence of the game will remain unchanged for eons to come.

# Glossary of Poker Terms

**Action:** The opportunity to act, requiring a player to check (pass), bet, raise, or fold.

**Ante:** A forced wager players are required to make before getting cards.

**All-in:** Betting all your chips or cash.

**Backdoor:** Catching both the turn and river cards to complete a drawing hand (also known as going runner-runner).

**Bad beat:** When a heavy, statistically favored hand is beaten by a lesser hand.

**Big blind:** The larger of the two blinds (forced bets) in Texas Hold'em, often double the small blind.

**Blank:** A card on the board that offers your hand no help or improvement.

**Blind:** A forced bet before the cards are dealt, usually posted by the two players immediately left of the button.

**Board:** The five community cards in Texas Hold'em (including flop, turn, and river).

**Brick and mortar:** Any real card room or casino where poker can be played.

**Button:** A marker—usually a white disk—indicating the dealer, the last player to act in a hand.

**Buy:** To steal a pot with a bluff.

**Buy-in:** The required entry fee for a tournament or minimum starting amount for a cash game.

**Call/call a bet:** Equaling the wager of a previous bettor.

**Catch:** To get the cards a player needs on a draw.

**Cardsharp:** An extremely skilled poker player (a.k.a. rounder or shark).

**Check:** A pass or nonbet.

**Check-raise:** An aggressive ploy in which a player checks, and when the action returns to him after a later player bets, he raises. Also referred to as trapping.

**Chop:** When players agree to split a tournament prize pool, or if no action preceded them, when they take back their blinds and go on to the next hand.

**Connectors:** Sequential cards.

**Counterfeit:** When board cards make a player's hand less valuable.

**Cowboys:** Pocket kings.

**Cut-off:** The position right before the button.

**Dead money:** A player in a tournament with little to no chance of winning.

**Dog:** Underdog.

**Donk/donkey:** A terrible poker player.

**Drag a pot:** Win a pot.

**Draw:** Attempting to complete or solidify a hand that will result in a strong hand.

**Drawing dead:** Playing a hand that will still not win the pot.

**Drawing thin:** Not as bad as drawing dead; designates that very few outs or cards will help you win a specific hand.

**Family pot:** When all (or most) of the players at the table call pre-flop.

**Felted:** To have lost all your chips or money. Busted.

**Fish:** A weak player. Not as bad as a donkey.

**Flop:** The first three community cards on the table.

**Flop on the cheap:** Getting to see the flop without having to call a big raise.

**Fold:** To throw your hand away and forfeit all money (if any) you have placed into the pot thus far; a.k.a. muck.

**Free card:** Seeing a card after the flop (turn or river) without having to call a bet courtesy of earlier aggressive play.

**Gutshot:** Making a straight by hitting an inside card.

**Heads-up:** Playing against one other player, in a single hand or in a full tournament.

**Hit:** When your cards connect or pair with the board cards, or if the board cards give you a strong hand.

**Hole cards:** In Hold'em, the two down cards (facedown cards) you are dealt.

**Hollywooding:** Acting; pretending that you don't have a strong hand or that you are confused about how to play your hand.

**Later street:** A later card or round.

**Limp/limp in:** To enter a pot without raising; to call.

**Made hand:** A completed hand; a hand that is not drawing.

**Muck:** To fold.

**No Limit:** A type of poker in which there is no maximum wager; players can bet everything they have in front of them at any time.

**Nuts:** The best possible hand based on the cards on the board.

**Offsuit:** Hole cards of two different suits.

**Outs:** Cards that make your hand the winner.

**Overpair:** A pocket pair higher than any card on the board.

**Pay-off:** Calling a bet, usually because of pot size, in a hand that you are probably behind and, if so, cannot win.

**Play the board:** When your hand is not stronger than the cards, or the hand, represented on the board.

**Pocket cards:** Hole cards. The two starting cards dealt to you facedown.

**Pocket pair:** Texas Hold'em starting hand consisting of paired cards.

**Pot-committed:** When the amount in the pot dictates that you call the final bet, even though there is a strong chance you cannot win because the pot is generally much larger than your stack.

**Pot Limit:** Unlike No Limit, in which you can bet anything in front of you, in Pot Limit the maximum bet is limited to what's already in the pot.

**Pot odds:** Amount of money already in the pot versus the amount you must put in to continue.

**Rags:** Ugly cards. Cards that have a low percentage for victory before the flop.

**Rake:** The amount of money taken from every pot for the house.

**River:** The final community card, also known as fifth street.

**Rock:** An extremely patient player.

**Runner-runner:** Catching both the turn and river cards to complete a drawing hand (a.k.a. backdoor).

**Second pair:** When your hand consists of the second highest card on the board.

**Semi-bluff:** When holding a drawing hand, this bluff—if called—can turn into a made (and very powerful) hand on a later street, assuming the right card or cards come.

**Set:** Trips, or three of a kind when you have a pair in your hand and catch one of the two remaining cards in the deck on the board.

**Short-stack:** Significantly less money or chips than the other players at the table.

**Slow-play:** Passively playing a big or strong hand in order to keep players in the pot.

**Small blind:** The smaller of the two forced bets or blinds.

**Stone-cold mortal lock:** An exaggerated term for the nuts.

**Suited:** In Hold'em, when your two hole cards are the same suit.

**Tell:** An unintentional clue or giveaway about a player's hand strength. Shaking hands, facial tics, and quickened breathing are all forms of tells.

**Throwing good money after bad:** Continuing to chase a losing hand (or a hand with a low percentage of victory). Better to cut your losses and fold.

**Tilt:** Wild or reckless play, usually resulting from a bad beat or other loss (a.k.a. go on tilt).

**Toke:** A tip for the dealer, usually from a player who has just won a hand.

**Turn:** The next up card (community card) after the flop, also known as fourth street.

**Ugly cards:** Rags; hole cards or starting cards that offer a low percentage of victory before the flop.

**Undercards:** Hole cards lower than the cards on the board.